What It Took to Come Home

How Covid Almost Killed Me, and Survival Changed Everything

What It Took to Come Home

How Covid Almost Killed Me, and Survival Changed Everything

By Kenneth Teter

A ventilator saved his life. Recovery changed it.

What It Took to Come Home

How Covid Almost Killed Me, and Survival Changed Everything

This book is a memoir based on the author's personal experience. Certain names, identifying details, and timelines may have been condensed or adjusted for narrative clarity while preserving the truth of events.

This book is not intended as medical advice, diagnosis, or treatment. It is a personal account of illness, survival, recovery, and perspective. Readers should consult qualified medical professionals regarding personal medical decisions.

First Edition
ISBN: 979-8-9961252-0-3
Printed in the United States of America

Dedication

To Amber—

my wife, my anchor, and the reason I found my way home.

To Jake and Lauren—

my children, my pride, and the future I fought to return to.

And in memory of my father,

Robert Lynn Teter,

August 3, 1947 – December 30, 2021

Staff Sergeant, United States Air Force

1965–1969

Vietnam Veteran

Author's Note

This book was never supposed to exist.

Like most people who survive something they do not fully understand while they are inside it, I assumed time would do what time usually does. I assumed it would soften the edges, quiet the memories, and eventually reduce the experience to something simpler than it was.

It didn't.

Time gave me distance, but it did not give me permission to forget.

What happened to me changed more than my health. It changed the way I see family. It changed the way I see work. It changed the way I see time, faith, medicine, trust, suffering, and what actually matters when life gets stripped down to its most basic truth.

Breath.

That is what this left me with.

Not fear.
Not bitterness.
Not a need to convince anyone of anything.

Just clarity.

This book was written because clarity has a responsibility attached to it.

I wrote it because memory softens things.
Because survival gets romanticized.
Because pain gets edited down by time.
Because people forget what it cost to come back once someone is standing in front of them again.

I wrote it because the truth matters.

Not the loud version.
Not the political version.
Not the version shaped to fit what people already want to believe.

Just the truth.

What happened.
What it cost.
What stayed.
What changed.
And what it gave back.

This is not a medical argument.
It is not a manifesto.
It is not an attempt to make my experience universal.

It is a record.

A record of what survival looked like.
A record of what recovery required.
A record of what became impossible for me to ignore once I lived through it.

If there is something I hope this leaves with you, it is not fear.

It is perspective.

Your time is not unlimited.
Your work is not your life.
The people waiting for you at home matter more than most of what

you spend yourself on.
The small things are not small.
And the life you are building is being shaped, every day, by what you keep choosing to prioritize.

That is what this gave me.

Not just another chance.

A clearer understanding of what to do with one.

Prologue — Before the Fall

Before COVID, before the hospital, before oxygen became something I had to think about, there was another room. Another uniform. Another moment where institutional certainty arrived dressed as fact and left no room for questions.

By the time COVID entered the world, I was already familiar with mandates.

I had spent nine years in the United States Air Force, serving in the Alabama Air National Guard with the 117th Air Transportable Hospital out of Birmingham. Drill weekends had their own rhythm—predictable, structured, and familiar in the way systems become familiar when you've lived inside them long enough. Roll call at 0800. Boots on tile. Fluorescent lights humming overhead. The smell of alcohol wipes, floor wax, and burnt government coffee hanging in the hallways before the day had even started. It was routine. Order. Repetition. Duty.

Military medicine had its own cadence. Clean. Hierarchical. Efficient. Everyone knew where they stood. Everyone knew how information moved. Some things came down formally. Others arrived earlier, passed quietly through hallways and break rooms before they ever became official.

That was how the first rumors started.

Not from the top.

From the edges.

By then, word had already started moving through units across the country. The Anthrax vaccine was coming. First in pieces. Rumors passed between medics, techs, and admin staff in half-finished conversations. Then more directly. Fertility concerns. Unusual reactions. Lingering symptoms. Enough to raise questions. Not enough to stop the machine.

Then it became official.

No long briefing. No open discussion. No room built for debate.

Just a quiet, direct message delivered the way institutional decisions usually are—cleanly, firmly, and without invitation.

The Anthrax vaccine would be mandatory.

Safe and effective.

That was the language.

Even then, I understood what mattered most was not the phrase itself, but the expectation beneath it.

Compliance first. Questions later.

Amber and I had already been talking about it for weeks by then. Not politically. Not emotionally. Practically.

We were trying to start a family. Nothing was wrong. No diagnosis. No fertility issues. Just two people in that quiet stretch of life where hope starts becoming planning. And the more we discussed it, the less comfortable I became with the idea of introducing something into my body under mandate with too many unanswered questions and too much institutional certainty surrounding too little actual transparency.

We were not anti-vaccine.

We were cautious.

That distinction mattered then, and it still does.

I was not refusing out of rebellion. I was not making a statement. I was making a calculation.

And the calculation was simple:

No institution was entitled to more confidence than the risk justified.

Not with my body.
Not with our future.
Not with consequences no one else would have to carry for me.

So I asked for a meeting.

Colonel Elliott was the hospital commander and a flight surgeon. Serious. Direct. Fair. The kind of man who understood hierarchy well enough not to hide behind it. I respected him, which made the conversation easier and harder at the same time.

I told him plainly: I was not taking the vaccine. I needed to know what my options were.

He did not lecture me.
Did not posture.
Did not try to sell me certainty.

He listened.

Then he gave me the cleanest answer available.

"If I were in your shoes," he said, "I'd resign."

There was no hostility in it. No punishment. No pressure.

Just clarity.

I asked him what that meant for my record. Whether I could leave clean. Whether I could still leave honorably.

His answer came just as plainly.

"You bring me the letter, I'll sign it."

So I did.

The next drill weekend, Saturday April 19, 1997 I turned in my resignation and finished the day like it was any other. Same halls. Same people. Same fluorescent lights. Same smell of stale coffee and disinfectant hanging in the air.

Then I walked out.

Nine years.
Gone in a single decision.

I drove home with the kind of silence that only follows choices you know were necessary and costly at the same time.

I felt relief.

I felt guilt.

I felt grief.

Relief because the decision was made.
Guilt because service had meant something to me.
Grief because walking away from something honorable can still feel like loss, even when leaving is the right decision.

I had loved the work.
I had loved the structure.
I had loved the service.

And I left anyway.

Not because I distrusted everything.

Because I had learned not to outsource judgment when the cost of being wrong becomes personal.

That lesson came two decades before COVID.

I do not begin here because this is a book about vaccines.

It is not.

I begin here because that moment taught me something I would carry into every room that followed: institutions can hold knowledge, authority, and skill, but they do not carry the consequences of your decisions for you.

That does not make institutions enemies.

It makes judgment personal.

By the time the next mandate arrived, the framework was already there.

PART I — THE DESCENT

01. The Slow Burn

It started quietly enough that I almost missed it.

Friday.

A full week and a day before I ever saw the inside of a hospital.

The day before, Thursday, I had been working. A normal day. Calls. Responsibilities. The usual rhythm. Nothing about it felt like a last normal moment — it just felt like another day I pushed through because that's what I did.

I didn't wake up sick on Friday. Not really. I woke up tired — the kind of tired that doesn't have a clean explanation. Not sore. Not feverish. Just… off. Like my body was running a half-second behind itself. I told myself it was nothing. I'd been busy. I'd been pushing. This was what tired felt like when you didn't listen to it soon enough.

By then, I was already in self-treatment mode, even if I didn't consciously label it that way. Fluids. Rest when I could manage it. Monitoring myself the way medical people do — detached, analytical, confident that experience counts for something. I wasn't alarmed. I was managing.

The PCR test came back positive, but even that didn't land the way it should have. The test was garbage — everyone knew it. It couldn't reliably distinguish between flu, cold, or COVID. A blunt instrument masquerading as certainty. I'd been at the clinic the day before I felt off, surrounded by nurses who were already out sick with COVID. Exposure wasn't a question. I noted the result and moved on.

For several days, I stayed sick — not dramatically, not desperately. Just consistently unwell. Fatigued. Run down. But breathing was still normal. Automatic. Something you don't think about until it demands attention.

Amber got sick the day after I did.

At first, it felt like parallel tracks — two people riding out the same thing side by side. But by Thursday, she was fully into it. Fevered. Wiped out. Clearly worse than she'd been earlier in the week. I noticed it, registered it, and still didn't connect it to what was happening in my own body.

That same Thursday — day six for me — I woke up feeling better.

Not healthy. Not strong. But improved. Enough that I crossed an invisible line in my head. The worst was behind me. That's how these things went. You felt bad, then you felt less bad, and eventually you moved on. I'd seen it before. I believed it.

Two days later, I woke up and couldn't breathe.

Not panic breathing. Not anxiety. Real air hunger — the kind that makes your chest feel shallow and wrong, like your lungs are only accepting partial permission. The kind that makes you sit upright without realizing you've done it.

That was the moment something shifted.

Not fear yet. Not urgency.

Just the quiet realization that my body was no longer following the plan I'd made for it.

02. The Herd

By the time we got to UAB, the decision had already been made.

That was the only part of the day that felt clear.

David had told me to get my ass to the hospital, and for once I listened without argument. Eight days after the first fatigue hit, Jake was driving me to Birmingham because breathing had become the one symptom I could no longer explain away.

The rest of it still felt uncertain.

I knew I was sick.
I knew I was short of breath.
I knew enough to be worried.

But I still did not understand how quickly concern had become consequence.

The first thing UAB took from us was the illusion that we were still in control of any of this.

When we pulled up to the emergency entrance, security was already outside directing traffic.

No parking.
No waiting.
No one comes in with you.

Drop-off only.

That was the rule.

Jake couldn't park and walk me in.
Couldn't help me check in.
Couldn't sit with me.
Couldn't even wait long enough for any kind of real handoff.

He had to drop me at the door and leave.

That was it.

No long conversation.
No pause.
No plan.
No reassurance.

Just the kind of abrupt separation that only happens when the system is already overwhelmed enough to stop pretending families matter in the intake process.

We barely got to say goodbye.

No hug.
No moment.
No real last look.

Just enough time to get out of the truck and close the door before he had to pull away.

Then I was alone.

That was the first real shift.

Up until then, this had still felt like something happening to us.

At the ER doors, it became something happening to me.

Inside was chaos.

That is the clearest word for it.

Not panic.
Not disorder.

Chaos.

The ER was packed in a way that did not feel temporary.

It felt saturated.

Like it had already been full for hours and had simply kept taking people anyway.

Every chair was filled.

Every wall had someone against it.

Wheelchairs were lined up with people slumped forward in them, masked and silent.

Patients sat on the floor.
Some leaned against walls.
Some stood because there was nowhere left to sit.
Some were already laid out on the floor trying to conserve what little energy they had left.

Everyone was masked.

Everyone was coughing.

Heads down.
Shoulders folded.
Breathing shallow.
Eyes half-open.

A few were already on oxygen.

Most looked like they were trying not to need it.

That was the first thing I noticed.

Not how sick I felt.

How many people looked exactly like I did.

That was the first real shock.

Not the positive test.
Not the shortness of breath.

The room.

The sheer number of us.

It had been one thing to be sick at home.

It was something else entirely to walk into a room full of people who looked like they had all made the same mistake at the same speed and arrived at the same point in the story.

That was where the disbelief set in.

Not panic.

Detachment.

Disbelief.

The room was too full to process emotionally, so my brain stepped sideways and observed it instead.

People in chairs.
People on floors.
People standing.
People coughing.
People waiting.

All of us arranged in rows and corners and overflow, waiting to be processed.

That was the feeling.

Not like patients.

Like cattle.

Rounded up.
Lined up.
Tagged.
Sorted.
Waiting our turn.

That was the herd.

Not because anyone was cruel.

Because there were too many bodies and not enough room for dignity.

That is what overflow looks like in a hospital.

It strips individuality first.

At triage, the nurse moved fast.

Not careless.
Fast.

She took the history.
Symptoms.
Duration.
COVID positive.
Shortness of breath.

Temperature.
Blood pressure.
Pulse ox.

Then she saw the oxygen saturation.

Eighty-eight.

That was the only number in the room that moved anyone faster.

The triage nurse immediately called for oxygen.

Nasal cannula.
Four liters.

That happened fast enough to tell me the number mattered, even if I still didn't fully understand how much.

Then it was back to the waiting room.

Wristband.
Paperwork.
Insurance.
Chair.

Wait.

That was the rhythm.

I was technically being treated now.

That didn't mean I had a room.

It meant I had oxygen and a place to sit while the system decided what to do with me.

The chair was hard plastic.

I felt it immediately.

Tailbone first.
Then hips.
Then lower back.

It was the kind of discomfort that becomes its own form of timekeeping.

Shift.
Sit.
Adjust.

Lean forward.
Try again.

Four hours in a hard plastic chair on four liters of oxygen while the ER churned around me.

That was the wait.

The oxygen didn't make me feel better.

That part mattered.

It didn't bring relief.
It didn't make breathing easy.
It didn't calm anything down.

It just kept me from getting worse.

At the time, that still felt like enough.

The room had a sound to it.

Coughing.
Constant coughing.

Not dramatic.
Not theatrical.

Just persistent.

Dry coughs.
Deep coughs.
Suppressed coughs.
The sound of people trying not to worsen what already hurt.

Nurses calling names.
Phones ringing.
Monitors chirping somewhere deeper in the unit.
Staff voices cutting through the noise in short, efficient bursts.

People answering questions too tired to answer well.
Someone crying.
Someone asking how much longer.
Someone coughing hard enough to stop the room for half a second.

It all blurred together.

Not silence.
Not noise.

Medical chaos.

And underneath all of it was the smell.

Bleach.
Alcohol.
Sanitizer wipes.
Disinfectant.

It smelled aggressively clean in the way hospitals do when they are losing ground and trying to sanitize faster than illness can spread.

That smell sat on everything.

By then, everyone in the room looked scared.

Not visibly panicked.

Something worse.

Exhausted enough to stop hiding it.

That was what the room held.

Not fear in motion.

Fear after energy.

People too depleted to perform anything but endurance.

And somehow that made it worse.

No one was dramatic.
No one was loud.

Just sick enough to know exactly why they were there.

I looked around and did what people always do in rooms like that.

I compared.

Who looked worse.
Who looked better.
Who was already on oxygen.
Who looked like they were really in trouble.

And because so many people looked worse than I thought I did, I minimized myself again.

That instinct almost never leaves.

I wasn't the worst one in the room.
So I must not be that bad.

Never mind the oxygen.
Never mind the sats.
Never mind the fact that I had already crossed a threshold I did not understand yet.

I blended in with the herd.

The only thing separating me from most of the room was the number on the monitor.

At some point they took me for a chest X-ray.

That was one of the stranger reassurances of the day.

Not clear.

Not normal.

But not the kind of fully blown, obvious bilateral pneumonia picture people expected either.

Not yet.

There were changes.
It wasn't clean.
But it wasn't catastrophic on film.

That gave everyone just enough ambiguity to keep moving without urgency.

Looking back, I understand that chest X-ray was one of the most misleading things in the room.

It lagged behind what was already happening in my lungs.

At the time, I didn't know that.

At the time, "not that bad yet" still sounded like safety.

It wasn't.

I texted Amber through the wait because it was the only way to stay connected.

She was one day behind me and sick with the same symptoms.

That part sat in the back of my mind the entire time.

I was in the ER.

She was at home, sick.

And all I could do was text updates between waiting and breathing and tell her the same thing I was only beginning to accept myself:

If this gets worse, come in.

The staff were clearly exhausted.

That was visible everywhere.

No one was careless.
No one was indifferent.

They were simply outnumbered.

The ER had that specific kind of strained efficiency that only shows up when everyone has been running too hard for too long and there is still nowhere near enough capacity for what keeps coming through the door.

The ICU felt more controlled when I finally got there.

The ER felt overwhelmed.

Four hours after they told me I was being admitted, someone finally came for me.

Not with a room.

With a wheelchair.

That was the transition.

Not because I needed the chair.
Because I was no longer waiting to see if I was staying.

I was being moved.

They told me they were admitting me.

There were no ER beds left.

Everything was full.

The only bed that had opened was one ICU bed outside the COVID unit.

One.

That was what I got.

The last bed.

I heard them say it as they moved me out.

At the time, I was grateful.

But I still did not understand what that sentence meant.

I heard it as logistics.

A lucky break.
A timing issue.
A bed opening.

I did not hear what it actually was.

A warning.

I was leaving the herd.

And I still did not understand why.

03. Watching Yourself Decline

There is a specific kind of denial that comes with knowing just enough medicine to be dangerous.

Not enough to save yourself.

Just enough to explain away what should alarm you.

That was the trap.

I had spent too much of my life around hospitals to romanticize them. Amber was an RN. Lauren was a CRNA. I had worked as an X-ray tech in the cath lab before spending the next thirty years in medical device. Between all of us, medicine was not abstract. Hospitals were not mysterious. Illness was not unfamiliar.

That should have made us quicker to react.

It made us more stubborn.

There is a particular arrogance that comes with proximity to medicine—not ego exactly, but a kind of quiet self-deception. You spend enough time around genuinely sick people and you start building internal thresholds. You tell yourself you know what bad looks like.

And because you know what bad looks like, you become convinced you are not there yet.

That was the lie.

I had spent enough time around real emergencies to believe I would know when this became one.

I believed that all the way up until I didn't.

By the middle of the week, the illness had changed shape.

It was no longer just fever and body aches and the miserable inconvenience of being sick.

It had become something heavier.

Not dramatic.
Not acute.
Just steadily worse.

That was what made it easy to ignore.

Nothing in it felt cinematic.

There was no single collapse.
No dramatic event.
No moment that looked like crisis.

Just visible decline in slow motion.

That was the danger.

You can rationalize a slow deterioration for far longer than you should.

The first place I could see it clearly was the bathroom mirror.

That became its own kind of checkpoint.

Not intentional.

Just habit.

Walk in.
Wash hands.
Catch your reflection.
Pause longer than you mean to.

At first it was subtle enough to dismiss.

By midweek it wasn't.

I looked sick.

Not tired.
Not run down.

Sick.

My skin had changed first.

The color was wrong.

Pale in a way that looked drained, but not cleanly pale.

Gray.

That was the word for it.

Not the kind of color that comes from fatigue.
The kind that makes you look older in a matter of days.

My face looked drawn.
My skin looked dull.
Everything in me looked depleted.

Sweat sat on me constantly.

Not the clean sweat of effort.
Fever sweat.

That damp, restless layer that never really leaves your skin and never lets you forget your body is burning through something.

And then there were my eyes.

Glassy.
Distant.
Older.

That was the part I noticed most.

I looked older in the mirror that week.

Not aged.

Diminished.

That was harder to explain away.

The mirror was the first place I had to confront the fact that I was not just sick.

I was visibly getting worse.

And still, I kept negotiating with it.

That was the strangest part.

You can look directly at your own decline and still refuse to name it correctly.

Amber saw it too.

Before either of us said it out loud, she was already watching the same things.

The fatigue.
The pauses.
The way my breathing had changed.

She could hear it before I admitted it.

Shallow breathing.
Longer pauses between sentences.
The quiet rhythm of someone trying not to sound winded.

She saw it.

I minimized it.

That became the rhythm of the week.

She watched.
I explained.

She noticed.
I dismissed.

Not because she didn't understand.

Because she was sick too.

That was part of what made the whole week harder to read clearly. We were both inside it. Both symptomatic. Both exhausted. There was no healthy observer standing outside the room calling the thing what it was.

Just two people in parallel decline, both still trying to convince themselves it was manageable.

By midweek, living inside my own body had become disorienting.

The best way I know to describe it is that it felt like an out-of-body experience without ever leaving my body.

I was still fully inside it.

Still aware.
Still conscious.
Still present.

But removed.

Not from what was happening.

From urgency.

That was the strangest part.

I could feel the decline.
I could see the decline.
I could register it clearly enough to observe it.

And still not react to it with the urgency it deserved.

It was like watching myself lose ground through fog.

The signals were there.

They just felt muted.

Everything slowed.

Thinking slowed.
Movement slowed.
Reaction slowed.

Even fear felt delayed.

That was what made it dangerous.

I was not unaware.

I was disconnected.

That illness fog did more than exhaust me.

It dulled my ability to assign the right level of consequence to what I was experiencing in real time.

I was watching myself decline without reacting to it.

That is real.

And it is harder to describe than pain.

Pain gets attention.

Decline does not.

Decline can feel strangely passive while it is happening.

That was what this felt like.

Not like crisis.

Like erosion.

By Thursday, weakness had finally caught up to everything else.

That was the first day my body started to feel hollow.

The fever had taken enough out of me.
The appetite was gone.
I had barely eaten all week.

I was forcing food because I knew I should.
Forcing fluids because I knew I had to.

Water.
Gatorade.
Small bites.
No appetite.
No instinct to eat.

Everything felt mechanical.

Drink this.
Eat something.
Try again later.

By then I could feel what not eating had done.

Not dramatically.

Just enough to notice the absence of reserve.

That was the feeling.

No reserve.

The body can tell when it has run through what it keeps in reserve for illness.

By Thursday, I could feel I was operating on less than I had.

That was the first day weakness stopped being abstract and became physical.

The clearest example was the shower.

Normally, a hot shower resets you.

Even sick, it helps.

It cuts the fever edge.
Clears your head.
Breaks the sweat.
Lets you feel human again.

That had always been the rhythm.

Feel terrible.
Shower.
Reset.

By Thursday, it didn't work.

I took the shower.
Got clean.
Stood there longer than I should have.
Let the heat hit.
Waited for the reset.

It never came.

I got out clean.

But I did not feel better.

That was new.

I felt cleaner.
Not well.

And worse than that, the shower exhausted me.

By the time I dried off, I was tired enough to lie down.

That was the first private moment that landed cleanly.

Not panic.
Not fear.

Recognition.

The shower didn't help.

That should have meant more to me than it did.

But even then, I translated it into something manageable.

I'm run down.
I need something stronger.
If this gets worse, I'll call.
If I feel bad enough, I'll get what I need and deal with it.

That was the next lie.

Not that I wasn't sick.

That I still controlled the timing.

That was how denial evolved.

It got quieter.
More informed.
More specific.

No longer:
I'll be fine tomorrow.

Now:
If this crosses the line, I'll know.

That was the version I believed by then.

Because I knew what bad looked like.

Because I had seen worse.

Because I still thought real danger would announce itself in a way I could not miss.

That was the mistake.

Real decline rarely announces itself.

It accumulates.

Quietly.
Gradually.
Persistently.

Until one day you catch yourself in the mirror looking pale and gray and older than you should, pausing between breaths, too tired to stand after a shower, watching yourself lose ground in plain sight—

and still calling it manageable.

It was the oldest trap in the world.

If you drop a frog in boiling water, it jumps.

But if you put it in the pot and raise the temperature slowly enough, it stays.

That was what this felt like.

Not collapse.

Acclimation.

Not crisis.

Gradual surrender.

I was watching myself lose ground in real time, slowly enough to normalize it, quietly enough to excuse it, and steadily enough to mistake decline for endurance.

By the time it felt dangerous, I had already been boiling for days.

04. The Last Bed

By the time they finally moved me out of the ER, it was close to two in the morning.

At that point, relief was simple.

Not because I thought I was better.

Because I was no longer in the chair.

Four hours in hard plastic under fluorescent light had reduced the immediate math of the night to something primitive: breathe, wait, shift, endure. By the time they came with the wheelchair, I was too tired to assign meaning to much beyond movement.

They were taking me somewhere else.

That was enough.

I still did not understand what "the last bed" meant.

Not really.

I had heard them say it in the ER.
Heard the phrase in passing as they moved me out.

One ICU bed.
Outside the COVID unit.
Last one available.

That was the first last bed — the one that got me out of the ER and into an ICU room outside the COVID unit.

Not the one Amber would later attach to the tattoo.

This one came out of the ER.

One ICU bed had opened, and it was enough to get me out of the herd.

At the time, it registered as logistics.

A capacity issue.
A timing issue.
A lucky break.

I heard it as a sentence about beds.

Not a sentence about how close the system already was to running out of places to put people like me.

That understanding came later.

At two in the morning, I was just relieved to be leaving the ER.

The ICU was quiet.

That was the first thing I noticed.

Not peaceful.

Not calm.

Quiet in the way serious places are quiet.

The ER had been noise and overflow and constant motion. The ICU felt controlled. The noise was lower, the movement more deliberate, the tone sharper. No one was rushing in the frantic way the ER had rushed. The pace was different here.

Not slower.

More precise.

That was the first real shift.

The ER had felt overwhelmed.

The ICU felt alert.

They wheeled me in, got me into bed, and started moving immediately.

No delay.
No waiting.
No "sit tight and we'll get to you."

That alone told me more than anyone said out loud.

The room itself was simple.

A bed.
Monitors.
A window.
Enough equipment to make it clear this was no longer temporary.

It wasn't dramatic. Just clinical in a different way. Less chaotic. More intentional.

The room had a view, but I barely registered it.

What I registered was the change in posture from the people around me.

The ER had felt like triage.

This felt like management.

A tech came in first and started getting me settled.

Vitals again.
Pulse ox again.
Blood pressure again.

The repetition alone told its own story.

No one here was assuming what the ER had already seen was enough.

They were starting over.
Rechecking everything.
Rebuilding the baseline.

Then they changed the oxygen.

The nasal cannula was gone.

They moved me to high-flow and immediately increased the support.

Eight liters.

That was the first number I remember in the ICU.

The jump mattered more than I understood in the moment.

The oxygen felt different immediately.

Not subtle.
Not comfortable.

Aggressive.

Dry air pushed hard and constant. The flow was stronger, louder, more mechanical. The head strap ran above my ears and sat just wrong enough to become its own source of irritation. It held the tubing in place, but every shift reminded me it was there.

It was not relief.

It was intervention.

That was the difference.

In the ER, oxygen had kept things from getting worse.

In the ICU, oxygen was already being adjusted to keep up.

That distinction took longer to fully land.

At the time, all I knew was that they had increased it, and no one in the room behaved like that was optional.

That was the first real sign the ICU staff gave me that we were no longer waiting to see.

They were already managing decline.

That was different.

The staff felt different too.

The ER had been exhausted.

The ICU was sharper.

More alert.
More immediate.
Less visibly strained, even if they were just as tired.

The urgency was quieter here, but it was more serious.

The ER had too many bodies and not enough room.

The ICU had fewer bodies and no wasted motion.

That distinction mattered.

Everything had a purpose.
Everything had a sequence.
Everything was already being watched.

They put me on telemetry.

That changed the room without changing the room.

Now I was being watched continuously.

Not checked.

Watched.

That was the first moment the shape of the situation started to shift, even if I still did not have the language for it.

The ER had observed me.

The ICU was tracking me.

That is not the same thing.

I texted Amber once I was in the room.

That was the first thing that mattered.

I finally had a bed.
They had moved me.
I was on high-flow now.
Eight liters.
I was going to try to sleep.

That was the message.

Practical.
Simple.
Measured.

Part update.
Part reassurance.

Mostly proof that I was still on the other end of the phone.

That was what mattered.

I took the first selfie sometime after they got me settled.

Not because I was scared yet.

Not because I was documenting anything for myself.

I took it for Amber.

Proof of life.
Proof of room.
Proof that I was still okay enough to send one.

That was all it was meant to be.

A quick visual update.
A way to show her where I was.
A way to reassure her that "admitted" still looked manageable.

That was the intention.

But the camera told a different story than my brain did.

That would become a pattern.

Over the next two days, I would take more.

Mostly to update her.
Mostly to show progression.
Mostly to stay connected to the people outside the room.

And in those pictures, the decline is obvious.

You can watch the oxygen go up.
Watch the face change.
Watch the color drain.
Watch the strain become visible.

At the time, I was still inside it.

Looking back, the camera was clearer than I was.

The numbers were already moving in the wrong direction.

The oxygen kept climbing to hold the saturation where they wanted it.

That was the trend that mattered.

Not how I felt.
Not what I thought.
Not what I hoped.

The sats.

That was the metric running the room now.

And the room responded to that number faster than I did.

That was the part I did not understand yet.

I still thought how I felt was the primary story.

The ICU already knew better.

They drew blood.
Then more blood.
Then arterial blood gases.

By then I was a human pin cushion.

But the blood draws themselves did not make it feel more serious.

The oxygen did.

The numbers did.

The way they watched the monitor did.

That was what changed the tone.

No one was waiting for me to say I felt worse.

They were watching it happen in real time.

That was new.

By then I was too exhausted to think much beyond the next hour.

The bed alone felt like relief after the ER chair.

That mattered more than it should have, but it was enough to matter.

For the first time since I had arrived, I could lie flat.
Stop shifting.
Stop bracing.
Stop enduring the chair.

I could rest.

That was enough to feel like progress, even if it wasn't.

That first night in the ICU was the first real pause since the ER.

Not because things were stable.

Because I was finally horizontal.

They came in and out through the night.

Vitals.
Blood.
Labs.
Adjustments.

But I slept.

Not well.
Not deeply.

But enough to disappear for stretches.

And at that point, disappearing for a while felt close enough to relief.

The ER had been uncertainty.

The ICU was escalation.

I just hadn't understood it yet.

And somewhere between the first high-flow adjustment and the first selfie, the room had already become more honest about what was happening than I was.

05. The Goodbye

By the time goodbye became real, no one called it that.

That was part of what made it so effective.

No ceremony.
No warning.
No dramatic last conversation where everyone says what they mean and understands what is happening in real time.

It arrived clinically.

At three in the morning.

By then I had already been in the ICU long enough to understand one thing clearly: the oxygen kept going up.

That was the trend that mattered.

I still did not understand the full shape of what was happening, but I understood enough to know the numbers were moving in the wrong direction and the room was responding to them faster each time.

That was the first warning.

The second came when the physician team walked in at three in the morning.

That hour alone told me something had changed.

Teams do not come into your room at three in the morning to tell you things are improving.

They came in direct.

No softening.
No easing into it.
No false reassurance.

Your oxygen saturation has hit a critical point.
This ICU can no longer manage you here.
We're moving you to the COVID unit.
We're going to have to intubate you.

That was the conversation.

It was clinical.
Clear.
Immediate.

And for a moment, none of it landed in the right order.

I understood the words.

I did not understand the threshold I had already crossed.

I knew I was sick.

I knew I was getting worse.

I knew breathing had become the center of the room.

But I still had not fully grasped that I had already moved beyond the point where effort and oxygen and time were enough to stabilize what was happening.

I had already passed that line.

I just hadn't understood it yet.

Intubate was not an abstract word to me.

I knew what it meant.

I had spent too much time around medicine not to.

I understood the mechanics.
The procedure.
The sequence.

What I did not understand in that moment was what it meant about me.

Not clinically.

Personally.

Intubation was no longer something that happened to other people in rooms I worked around.

It was now what was about to happen to me.

That was the first moment the room changed.

Not medically.

Existentially.

Everything before that still carried some version of implied return.

Treatment.
Monitoring.
Escalation.
Intervention.

All of it still carried the quiet assumption that I was sick, but still fundamentally on the same side of the line as everyone standing around me.

Intubation changed that.

It was the first moment the situation stopped feeling like treatment and started feeling like surrender.

Not emotional surrender.

Physiologic surrender.

My body was losing the argument.

That was what the room was actually telling me.

And for the first time since I walked into UAB, I understood enough to feel the weight of it without yet understanding all of its consequences.

That was the moment goodbye became real.

Not because anyone said I might die.

Because everyone in the room was suddenly moving like that possibility had entered the conversation whether anyone named it or not.

I texted Amber first.

That part was automatic.

I did not call anyone else.
I did not make a plan.
I did not think through sequence.

I texted Amber.

That was instinct.

I told her they were moving me to the COVID unit.
I told her they were going to intubate me.
I told her I would call her.

Even then, the shape of the message was protection.

Information first.
Reassurance second.
Truth, but only enough of it to be useful.

I was trying to tell her what was happening without making her carry what I was only just beginning to understand myself.

That was the instinct.

Contain it.
Control it.
Keep everyone else steady.

I told her I was going to be okay.

I did not know if that was true.

I told her anyway.

That was the line I could still offer her.

Not certainty.

Just something less terrifying than silence.

They moved me to the COVID unit.

That was the second last bed.

The first one had gotten me out of the ER and into an ICU room outside the COVID unit.

This one was different.

This was the COVID unit.

This was the room they were moving me to because I was headed for intubation.

And this was the one Amber would come back to later.

Not that night.

Not while everything was still moving too fast to understand.

Later.

It was the tattoo on my arm.

A bald eagle wrapped in the American flag.

The words beneath it: Freedom Isn't Free.

I had gotten it long before COVID, long before UAB, long before the COVID unit and the second last bed became part of our story. It was not decoration to me. It was memory. Service. Cost. Country. My father. My own years in uniform. The kind of phrase people say easily until life makes them understand that freedom, survival, family, and breath all come with a price.

That day, the news was full of Afghanistan.

Troops coming out.

Images none of us could stop watching.

A country arguing over what service had cost and what leaving meant.

And somewhere inside that hospital, I was being moved into the last available bed in the COVID unit.

Amber has always believed that tattoo mattered.

Not medically.

Not officially.

Not in a way anyone could prove.

But she believes someone saw it.

Saw the eagle.

Saw the flag.

Saw those words.

Saw a man who had served, a man with a family waiting outside a hospital they could not enter, and decided that if there was one COVID bed left, he was getting a chance.

I do not know if that is true.

I cannot prove it.

I would never claim I could.

But I know this: when you survive something that close, the people who love you search for meaning in every detail. They look for mercy wherever they can find it. They replay the timing, the faces, the decisions, the small things that may have mattered when everything was hanging by a thread.

For Amber, that tattoo became part of the story.

The eagle.

The flag.

Freedom Isn't Free.

The COVID unit.

The second last bed.

Maybe it was coincidence.

Maybe it was grace.

Maybe it was just the system making the best decision it could in the middle of a night when there were too many bodies and not enough rooms.

I do not know.

But I understand why she believes it.

Because from her side of the hospital walls, she could not hold my hand. She could not speak to the doctors in person. She could not see the room. She could not watch over me. So she held on to the one thing she could see clearly in her mind: that somehow, in a hospital full of dying people, I was given the last COVID bed at the moment I was about to disappear.

And on my arm were the words I had carried for years.

Freedom Isn't Free.

That was where the reality of it sharpened.

The ICU had been escalation.

The COVID unit was consequence.

We FaceTimed right before they intubated me.

That was the real goodbye, even if neither of us had the language to call it that.

She was crying.

Not controlled.
Not composed.

Crying the way people cry when they are already searching your face for answers you do not have and can see fast enough that you are too far inside it to give them any.

She wanted answers.

I did not have them.

She wanted reassurance.

I was trying to manufacture it in real time.

I told her I loved her.

I told her I was going to be okay.

That was what I gave her.

Not because I believed it fully.

Because it was all I had to give.

I did not say goodbye.

I did not say what I was actually thinking.

I did not say that I understood enough to know this had become dangerous in a way it had not been an hour earlier.

I did not say that I was scared.

I did not say that I was trying very hard not to let the fear become visible on my face.

I did not say that I knew enough medicine to understand why people started speaking to me in this tone when outcomes were no longer assumed.

I did not say that part out loud.

I told her I loved her.

That was the closest thing to truth I could say cleanly.

I was not calm.

I do not remember sounding calm, and I know now I could not have looked it.

By then I was struggling to breathe hard enough that calm had become performance.

I was drowning slowly enough to still speak, and that is a terrible place to be because it lets everyone pretend speech still means safety.

It does not.

I was trying to reassure her while fighting for enough air to finish the sentence.

That was the conversation.

She was crying.
I was trying to sound steadier than I was.
Neither of us had enough information to name what was happening correctly, but both of us knew enough to understand this was no longer routine.

I was protecting her.

And the kids.

That was the instinct underneath everything else.

Not bravery.

Containment.

Keep the fear from spreading faster than the facts.

That was the role.

That was what I knew how to do.

Then the doctor took my phone.

That was the moment it became real.

Not because anyone said I might die.
Not because anyone said goodbye.
Not because I suddenly understood everything that was about to happen.

Because they took my phone out of my hand, and whatever came next was no longer mine to manage.

That was the last piece of control I had.

I told Amber I loved her.
I told her I was going to be okay.
The doctor told her they would take good care of me.

Then they took my phone away.

And the next thing I knew, I was waking up seven days later.

Interlude — After the Phone Went Quiet

Amber's version of that night did not end when mine did.

Mine disappeared into sedation.

Hers continued in silence.

The phone call ended, the screen went dark, and she was left with the last image of my face before the tube. No room to sit in. No hand to hold. No nurse to stop in the hallway. No way to ask the next question and read the answer in someone's eyes.

COVID did that to families.

It did not only isolate patients.

It isolated fear.

She had to carry the unknown from outside the room. She had to tell the kids what could be told without saying everything that might be true. She had to wait for updates from people she could not see, about a husband she could not touch, in a hospital she could not enter.

I was unconscious.

She was not.

That is one of the things I understand differently now. The ventilator took seven days from me. It did not take them from her.

PART II — THE DISTANCE

06. Seven Days Gone

The next thing I knew, I was waking up seven days later.

Not all at once.

Not cleanly.

Not in the way people wake in movies—eyes open, memory intact, immediate understanding.

I came back in fragments.

Consciousness did not return like a switch.

It leaked in.

In pieces.
In flashes.
In partial awareness that never arrived in the right order.

The first thing I remember—if memory is even the right word for it—was that I was tied to the bed.

That was the first shape of awareness.

Not the room.
Not the tube.
Not the machines.

Restraints.

Hands and feet.

That was the first thing my mind could make sense of, and even then it made no sense at all.

I did not understand why I could not move.

I do now.

At the time, I did not.

At the time, it felt less like medicine and more like captivity.

Not because I thought anyone was hurting me.

Because I was awake enough to recognize I was trapped and still too sedated to understand why.

That is a specific kind of terror.

Not panic.

Something slower.

Confusion with nowhere to go.

I was too sedated to be fully awake.
Too aware to stay unconscious.
Too restrained to do anything but remain inside it.

That was the space I came back into.

I was not in pain.

That part surprised me later.

Not because nothing hurt.

Because I was still too heavily sedated for pain to become the dominant signal.

I was confused.
Weighted.
Chemically distant from my own body.

Everything felt blurred, out of focus, slowed by something heavy and artificial.

My mind was trying to solve a puzzle with missing pieces while still half-buried under whatever they had used to keep me still enough to survive.

Nothing arrived clearly.

Nothing arrived in sequence.

Thought was fragmented.
Time was gone.
Cause and effect had separated.

I knew I was breathing.

I did not know how.
I did not know why.
I only knew something was doing it for me.

That was the first deeper wrongness.

Breath was happening.

But it did not belong to me.

By the time I was awake enough to recognize the tube, I knew enough to understand what it was.

I was intubated.

That realization did not arrive with panic.

It arrived with recognition.

And recognition was worse.

Because recognition meant context.

Context meant consequence.

I did not know how long I had been there.
I did not know what day it was.
I did not know what had happened between the phone leaving my hand and this.

I only knew I was still here.

And I was no longer in control of my own body.

The room was dark.

Not black.

Dim.

The television was the only real light in the room.

The glow from it washed everything in low color and shadow and made the entire room feel suspended somewhere between dream and sedation.

That was the atmosphere I came back into.

Dark room.
Low light.
Tube.
Restraints.
Half-consciousness.

And the television.

That was the strangest mercy in the room.

Classic rock was playing.

Not loud.
Not intrusive.

Just there.

Soft enough to drift in and out of consciousness with.

The music was the first familiar thing I found.

38 Special.
Toto.
Duran Duran.
Kansas.
Journey.

Songs I knew.
Songs I recognized.
Songs that belonged to a world outside that room.

That mattered more than it should have.

The music grounded me.

It was the only thing in the room that felt normal.

Every twenty or thirty minutes, the screen would flash the words peace, tranquility, and love before dropping back into the music videos.

Just long enough to register.
Then gone.

Back to the songs.

It was surreal.

Drugged, restrained, intubated, half-buried in sedation and trying to determine if I was in a hospital room, in hell, or somewhere between the two—and the only stable thing in the room was classic rock and those three words cycling through the dark like a signal from somewhere I could still reach.

That mattered.

It tethered me.

The hallucinations came with everything else.

Voices.
Shadows.
Dark figures at the edges of the room.

Not dreams.

Not exactly.

They were too present for that.

Sedation blurred everything into something between nightmare and reality. The room was full of things that felt real enough to react to and impossible enough to know they weren't.

There were shapes in the corners.
People who were not there.
Dark forms moving where nothing should have been moving.

At one point, the sharps container had a face.

A cartoon face.

It looked like a cake.
It spoke.
It watched me.

That is what the drugs did.

Not enough consciousness to orient.
Too much to escape it.

The body was worse.

Or stranger.

I did not feel like I was in my body.

I felt trapped inside a vessel that belonged to me only in the most technical sense.

I knew it was mine.

I just did not feel attached to it.

That was the hallucination beneath all the others.

Not just that the room was wrong.

That I was.

I was trapped inside something I recognized but could not control.

That may be the strangest feeling I have ever known.

Not pain.
Not fear.

Dislocation.

I did not panic.

That still surprises people when I say it.

But I didn't.

I was too sedated to panic properly.

Too confused to organize fear into something sharp enough to become panic.

What I felt most was confusion.

And uncertainty.

Not fear in the active sense.

Just the slow, crushing uncertainty of not knowing what had happened, where I was inside it, or whether any of this was moving toward recovery or somewhere else entirely.

That was the emotional center of waking up.

Not terror.

Uncertainty.

The first person I remember clearly was my nurse.

I was awake enough by then to understand one thing clearly:

I needed her to call my wife.

That became the first coherent thought.

Not where am I.
Not what happened.
Not how long.

Call Amber.

That was the first thing in me that came back intact.

I could not speak.

The tube made that impossible.

I could not move much either.

But I was awake enough to try.

I made small hand motions.

She leaned in.

I air-wrote with my finger, trying to form words in space I could not say out loud.

She watched me do it for a second, then asked if I wanted a pen and paper.

I nodded.

She put them in my hand.

I tried to write.

What came out was barely a letter.

A broken shape.
A rough curve.
A makeshift C.

That was all I could manage.

And somehow it was enough.

She looked at it once and asked, immediately, if I wanted her to call Amber.

I nodded.

And nearly lost it.

That was the first real emotional break.

Not waking up.
Not the restraints.
Not the tube.

Recognition.

One broken letter.

One scribbled C.

And suddenly I was no longer just a body in the bed.

I was awake enough to be understood.

Briefly.
Poorly.
Barely.

But enough.

Enough to communicate.
Enough to be recognized.
Enough to be heard.

Enough to know I was still in there.

And above all else—

alive.

07. Vent Dreams

The drugs did not take me nowhere.

They took me inward.

That was the first thing I understood later, once enough of the sedation burned off to separate memory from chemistry.

What happened on the ventilator did not feel like dreaming.

Dreams imply distance.
A layer.
A softness.
Something symbolic enough to survive waking.

This was not that.

None of it felt like sleep.

It felt like reality with the wrong architecture.

That was what made it so convincing.

Nothing in it felt invented while I was inside it.

It felt revealed.

Not dreams.

Judgment.

That was the shape of it.

Not random hallucination.
Not meaningless noise.

Something harsher.

The drugs made the room unstable, but what came through it did not feel random.

It felt personal.

The most persistent thing in the room was the girl.

She never moved.

Not once.

Always in the same place.

Curled up on the wall.
Naked.
White skin.
Long black stringy hair hanging over her face and shoulders.
Thin in the way sick things are thin.
Still in the way dead things are still.

Just watching me.

That was all she ever did.

She never lunged.
Never spoke.
Never moved toward me.

She just watched.

Curled there on the wall, staring at me like she knew something I didn't.

That was what made her worse.

Not violence.

Judgment.

She did not feel overtly evil.
Not exactly.

Not demonic in the way movies teach you to imagine demons.

Something quieter.

Something more clinical.

She felt judgmental.

Not cruel.
Not kind.

Just there.

Watching.

Measuring.

There was something almost neutral in her, which made it worse.

But she did not feel like fear.

She felt like witness.

That was harder to survive.

I still do not know why she was naked.
Why she looked like that.
Why it was a girl.
Why the hair.
Why the wall.

I do not know whether she was a demon, an angel, or something in between.

I only know she felt like judgment given shape.

And she stayed there for days.

The drugs kept the room unstable, but she remained constant.

That was what made her real.

Everything else shifted.

She did not.

That mattered.

The rest came in fragments.

Voices.
Shadows.
Distortions at the edges of the room.
Dark figures where nothing should have been.

But the deeper hallucinations were not visual.

They were emotional.

The room lied.

The mind did not.

That was the real horror of it.

The sedation distorted the room, but it stripped the rest of me bare.

The drugs did not create regret.

They removed the filters that usually keep it manageable.

That was what came through.

Not fear first.

Regret.

It came like a film reel.

Specific scenes.

Specific absences.

The things I had missed.
The things I had delayed.
The things I had told myself would still be there later.

Lauren's dances.
Jake's practices.
The dinners missed.
The date nights skipped.
The weeks spent working when I should have been home.

That was the reel.

A life audit.

Scene after scene with all the emotional weight still attached.

That was what made it unbearable.

You did not just remember it.

You felt it again.

The missed moments.
The wrong priorities.
The quiet substitutions you justify while you are busy and successful and convinced provision is the same thing as presence.

That illusion does not survive a ventilator.

The fear underneath all of it was simple.

I may never see them again.

Not death in the abstract.

Absence.

That COVID had made visitation impossible sharpened everything.

Not death.

Separation.

The house was in there too.

Lake Trace.

The house we built.
The house none of us wanted to sell.
The life we had already been forced to let go of.

That was another thing the ventilator stripped clean.

Money had no persuasive power there.

None.

The sharps container talked to me.

It looked like a cake.

And we talked.

Not out loud.

Mentally.

I could not speak.
I was intubated.

But it heard me anyway.
Answered anyway.

Full conversations.

And then slowly, as the sedation wore off, the room began to return.

The girl on the wall became a computer desk bolted into place.

The talking cake became the sharps container in the corner.

The dark room became a hospital room again.

Reality reassembled itself in pieces.

That should have been comforting.

It wasn't.

The room had lied.

The regrets did not.

The drugs made the room lie.

But the regrets were real.

08. The Pull Back

Reality didn't come back all at once.

It corrected itself.

Slowly.
Reluctantly.
In pieces.

The first crack in the hallucinations wasn't clarity.

It was contradiction.

The girl on the wall didn't disappear.

She changed.

One moment she was there—curled, watching, silent.

The next, she wasn't gone.

She was a desk.

Bolted to the wall.
Still.
Inanimate.
Exactly where she had always been.

The same thing happened with the sharps container.

The cake didn't vanish.

It resolved.

Plastic.
Stationary.
Ordinary.

That was the moment something shifted.

Not because everything made sense.

Because something stopped lying.

The room came back first.

Not fully.

But enough.

Edges sharpened.
Shapes held still.
Objects stayed what they were from one moment to the next.

That was new.

For days, nothing had held its form.

Now it did.

That was the first sign I was coming back.

The people took longer.

At first, they were still just movement.
Voices.
Presence without identity.

It took a couple of days for them to become people again.

Not because they changed.

Because I did.

The sedation was wearing off, and with it went the distortion that had flattened everything into shadows and fragments.

Faces became faces.
Voices became voices tied to someone standing in the room.

And with that came something else.

Understanding.

Not full understanding.

But enough to know I had been gone.

It didn't arrive as a timeline.

It arrived as absence.

There was a gap I couldn't fill.

Days that had happened without me.

That realization didn't scare me.

It just sat there.

Unanswered.

By then I was still intubated.

Fully aware enough to think.
Aware enough to understand what the tube was doing.

And aware enough to know I couldn't touch it.

They watched me closely.

That was clear.

Not because they said it.

Because of how they moved.

Always aware of my hands.
Always aware of my awareness.

They were waiting for me to be lucid enough to trust.

Not yet.

That was the line.

I was present.

But not trusted.

Not fully.

That space—awake but restricted—should have been frustrating.

It wasn't.

It just was.

By then, everything felt like it was unfolding the way it needed to.

That was the strange part.

There was no resistance in me.

No fight against the process.

No urgency to change it.

Just movement in one direction.

Back.

The first real physical discomfort came from something simple.

My stomach.

The cramping.

All the medication, the laxatives—they had done what they were supposed to do, but the result was constant discomfort.

Not sharp pain.

Persistent.

Unavoidable.

The kind of discomfort that reminds you your body is still there, still working, still reacting.

That was one of the first things that felt real.

The rest of my body came back slower.

My legs were the first I felt clearly.

Not strength.

Awareness.

They were there.

Heavy.
Weak.
But mine again.

They were working to keep them that way.

Lovenox injections in my stomach.
Blood thinners to prevent clots.

Even that became part of the rhythm.

Another sign that I was still here.

Still being maintained.

Still being pulled back.

The restraints stayed on for most of that time.

Until the day before they extubated me.

That mattered more than I expected.

Not because I wanted to move.

Because it meant something had changed.

They trusted me enough to let me have my hands back.

That was progress.

Not something I felt.

Something they knew.

Communication came back before speech.

Pen.
Paper.

That was how I asked for things.

The first requests were simple.

Ice chips.

My mouth was dry in a way that is hard to explain.

Not just thirsty.

Stripped.

The ice wasn't about hydration.

It was relief.

Something cold.
Something real.
Something that felt normal in a body that hadn't felt normal in days.

The next thing was my teeth.

I wanted them brushed.

Not for hygiene.

For dignity.

I felt dirty.

Not physically.

Internally.

And brushing my teeth felt like the first step back to being human again.

Small things.

But they mattered more than anything else in that moment.

That's what returning feels like.

Not big realizations.

Small corrections.

One thing at a time.

There was no single nurse that stands out.

But there was a connection.

One of Lauren's classmates was there.

Working in the COVID unit.

That mattered.

Not because of what she did.

Because she was tied to something outside that room.

A bridge.

Proof that my life still existed somewhere beyond monitors and machines.

Time didn't come back cleanly either.

It stayed fractured.

Blurry.

Even when they asked me what day it was, I couldn't answer.

The board was there.

The date was written.

I couldn't read it.

I could have looked at my phone.

But even that was a problem.

My hands shook.

Not slightly.

Enough that even holding the phone and trying to type felt like work.

That was when I realized how much had been taken from me physically.

Not dramatically.

Just enough to make everything harder.

The first real emotional shift wasn't fear.

It was relief.

I was still here.

That was it.

No deeper analysis.
No big realization.

Just that.

Alive.

Before I was extubated, Lauren came in.

That was the moment everything changed.

She held my hand.

And I lost it.

Not quietly.

Not controlled.

Emotion broke through everything else.

That was the first moment I knew I was going to be okay.

Not because someone told me.

Because I could feel it.

Connection.

Presence.

Reality.

All of it back in one moment.

That mattered more than anything the monitors were saying.

The next day, they told me something I didn't understand yet.

I was the first patient to come off the ventilator since July 1st.

It was now September 1st.

At the time, it didn't land.

It sounded like information.

A statistic.

Something worth noting, but not something I could feel.

That would come later.

In the moment, it didn't change how I felt.

I was still in the bed.
Still recovering.
Still trying to piece together what had happened.

The weight of that statement didn't hit until I was discharged.

Until I understood what it meant to be the only one.

But in that room, in that moment, it was just another piece of information in a body still trying to return to itself.

Pulling back didn't feel dramatic.

It felt natural.

Like something that was always supposed to happen.

No resistance.
No fight.

Just movement.

Forward.

Out.

Back into something recognizable.

I was still weak.
Still tubed.
Still limited.

But the room had stopped lying.

And that was enough.

09. First Air

They spent thirty minutes preparing me to breathe before they let me try.

That was the first thing that mattered.

Extubation was not dramatic.

It was deliberate.

Measured.
Controlled.
Prepared for.

By the time they were ready to pull the tube, the room had already decided what came next.

They hyperoxygenated me first.

Thirty minutes of preparation.
Thirty minutes of making sure my body had enough reserve to survive what came after the tubes came out.

That was the part I did not understand in real time.

Extubation did not mean I was stable.

It meant they believed I might be stable enough to try.

That is not the same thing.

By then I knew enough to understand what was coming.

I had been awake long enough to know what was in my throat.

Not just the ventilator.

That was the surprise.

It was not one tube.

It was several.

The vent tube.
A gastric tube beside it.
Other lines and support I could feel but could not name.

More than I expected.
More than I had imagined.

That was what I remember most.

Not one tube leaving.

The sheer amount of what had been inside me.

They explained what they were going to do.

Step by step.

What to expect.
What I would feel.
What they needed from me.

Then they started pulling.

It felt exactly like what it was.

Too many things coming out of too small an opening.

Not pain exactly.

Pressure.
Friction.
Volume.

You could feel the fullness of it on the way out.

The shape of everything leaving at once.

It was not violent.

But it was not easy either.

The extubation itself was rough enough to make it memorable.

Not traumatic.

Just physical in a way only something that invasive can be.

Then it was out.

And I coughed.

Not hard.
Not violently.

Just enough to know the breath was mine again.

That was the first proof.

The coughing mattered.

Not because it hurt.

Because it was mine.

That first breath came easier than I expected.

That surprised me.

After all of it, I expected breathing to feel foreign.

Borrowed.
Fragile.
Tentative.

It didn't.

It felt natural.

I coughed.
Adjusted.
Breathed.

And the breath came.

That was the first quiet miracle of it.

Not that it was easy.

That it was mine.

They had high-flow ready the second the tubes came out.

That part mattered too.

The support was still necessary.

This was not freedom.

It was transition.

The ventilator was gone.

The oxygen was not.

High-flow took over immediately.

Not as backup.

As necessity.

My sats still hovered just above ninety-one.

That was enough to survive.

Not enough to pretend I was out of danger.

That mattered.

Extubation was not the finish line.

It was the end of the first emergency.

That was all.

The first thing I wanted was water.

Not food.
Not my phone.
Not answers.

Water.

That instinct overrode everything else.

My mouth was dry in a way that felt structural.

Not thirst.

Damage.

Days of tubes and dry air had stripped everything raw.

I wanted water immediately.

They brought ice chips instead.

That was not caution.

That was mercy.

I still could not swallow properly.

That part came next.

The tube was gone.
The breathing was mine.

Swallowing was not.

That was its own kind of surprise.

Occupational therapy had to help me relearn it.

We started with ice.
Then thicker liquids.
Then things designed to coat the throat enough to make swallowing possible again.

The mechanics had to be taught back.

That was humbling.

Jello came next.

And it was fantastic.

Not because it was food.

Because it was progress.

Then soda.
Then juice.
All of it staggered.
All of it earned.

One small thing at a time.

That was recovery now.

Not milestones.

Permissions.

I tried to speak.

Nothing came out.

That part had been expected.

They had warned me.

Still, expectation and experience are not the same thing.

The first words did not come as words.

They came as breath trying to become sound and failing.

Whisper first.
Then fragments.
Then something close enough to speech to count.

I do not remember the exact first words.

Something practical.

Probably where my phone was.

Something ordinary.

That felt right.

After all of that, ordinary was the first thing I wanted back.

My throat stayed sore for days.

Raw.
Tender.
Unreliable.

My voice took time.
My swallow took time.

None of that surprised the staff.

They had prepared me for all of it.

That helped.

What I was not prepared for was everyone else.

Once the tube was out, people started coming in.

Not just staff assigned to me.

People came to see.

Doctors.
Nurses.
Respiratory.
Staff from the unit.

They came in because I was the only patient to come off the ventilator in three months.

That was the part I did not understand then.

Not really.

To me, it was just another moment in a room I was still trying to survive.

To them, it was something else.

Doctors were crying.

I remember that more clearly now than I did then.

Not because I understood it in the moment.

Because I didn't.

At the time, I was too close to it to understand what they were seeing.

To me, it was extubation.

To them, it was survival.

That difference would not land until much later.

The relief was physical first.

Then emotional.

First the breath.
Then the understanding that the breath was mine.
Then the weight of what that meant.

I had survived the first part.

That was all I knew.

Not that I was safe.
Not that I was healed.
Not that I understood what came next.

Only that I had made it through the first part alive.

And for that moment, that was enough.

The first cold ice chip in my mouth was the first thing that felt like life returning.

10. The Second Descent

They said I was improving.

Stable enough to leave COVID ICU.

They moved me to a step-down unit — just a hallway over, but it felt like miles. New room. New bed.

Less equipment. Same oxygen — 15 liters per minute, high-flow — but no more constant alarms, no more ceiling-mounted arms and trauma carts within reach.

It should've felt like progress.

But the silence in the new room was different.

Not restful.

Exposed.

The nurses came in less often. Monitors weren't as close. I was breathing on my own now, technically — though without the high-flow oxygen line, I was sure I wouldn't last five minutes.

I scrolled my phone. Blinked through messages. Tried to type. My hands still shook. Still lagged. But they worked.

I was starting to feel human again.

Until I couldn't breathe.

It happened fast — and not fast.

I noticed a strange tightness in my chest first. Then a throb behind my eyes. My ears started ringing.

The world narrowed.

I looked at the oxygen line.

It was still in my nose.

Still strapped behind my ears.

Still humming.

But something felt off.

Then the pulse oximeter alarmed.

Low 80s.

Then 70s.

A tech down the hall saw the numbers drop on her monitor and called it in.

I remember the door bursting open.

At least four people came in — two nurses, a respiratory therapist, someone else I didn't recognize.

I couldn't speak.

I just gripped the bedrails and stared.

They moved fast — pulling open cabinets, checking vitals, inspecting the oxygen unit.

Then someone followed the line all the way to the wall and stopped.

"It's not connected."

Silence.

Everyone froze for a second.

My oxygen line — the only thing keeping my blood oxygen from crashing — had come unplugged from the wall.

No alarm. No alert.

Just a silent drift into suffocation.

I saw one nurse glance at the other, guilt mixing with panic.

The respiratory therapist reattached the line.

The hiss of oxygen returned.

Within seconds, I felt the cold air flood my nostrils again. My chest began to rise deeper. The pressure behind my eyes eased. My hearing returned in layers.

I was breathing again.

But differently this time.

Shaky. Untrusting. Alert.

They rushed me back to COVID ICU "just to be safe."

That's what they said.

But we all knew the truth.

They'd nearly lost me again.

Not to the virus. Not to organ failure. Not to infection.

To a plug in a wall.

A simple mistake.

The kind that kills people.

They moved fast, professionally. I could see the fear behind their movements.

I wanted to be angry.

But I was too tired.

Too terrified.

But I was different now.

Something in me had cracked.

And that crack made room for something colder: doubt.

I didn't know who was watching over me.

I only knew this — I had to watch over myself.

Even when I couldn't.

The room looked exactly like the first one. Same walls. Same lights. Same looping alert tones. But it wasn't the same.

I wasn't the same.

This time, I wasn't unconscious.

I was wide awake — and terrified.

They moved fast when I came in. Another ICU nurse hooked me back to the monitors. The respiratory therapist re-checked the oxygen settings. They scanned every tube, every wire. This time, they weren't trusting anything.

I was upright now, slightly propped, my chest heaving under the high-flow mask. The cool air blasted into my nostrils like wind through a tunnel. I tried to slow my breathing, but it wasn't just my lungs reacting — it was me.

I was scared.

And the staff knew it.

One of the nurses — I think her name was Shelby — stood by the vitals monitor a little longer than usual. Her eyes didn't match her voice.

"You're okay," she said. "Numbers look better already."

But I could see her watching the pulse ox. Watching me. Watching the oxygen line like it might leap out of the wall again.

There was an edge to everything now. They were careful. Not cautious — careful. Like someone handling glassware after a drop. No one said it out loud, but I saw it on their faces: We nearly lost this one.

I stared at the wall.

Not the corner where the goth girl once sat.

Not the cartoon-faced cake.

Just the blank wall. Beige. Seam line down the middle. A little scuff near the outlet.

It was the most honest thing in the room.

I felt rage in my chest — not at them, not even at what happened — but at how helpless I was. One plug comes loose and I nearly die. One slip, and I'm right back where I started.

I didn't want to cry.

Didn't want them to see.

But it came anyway.

Slow tears. No noise. Just wet on the pillow.

They pretended not to notice.

Or maybe they really didn't.

Maybe they were crying somewhere too.

I lay there for hours, staring at that wall. Blinking. Breathing. Listening.

Machines beeped softly. Feet passed in the hallway. The HVAC hummed overhead.

Alive.

Still.

But not safe.

11. The Mirror

The first time I saw myself clearly, it wasn't in a mirror.

It was in the front-facing camera of my phone.

That felt appropriate.

Not reflection.

Documentation.

By then I was stable enough to hold the phone, which was its own kind of milestone, even if my hands still shook enough to make the frame unsteady. I wasn't strong. I wasn't steady. But I was upright enough, aware enough, and curious enough to finally look.

That was the threshold.

Not recovery.

Recognition.

I didn't take the picture because I was vain.
I took it because I needed proof.

Proof of what had happened.
Proof of what was left.
Proof that the person on the other side of all of this was still me.

That was the intention.

Not vanity.

Documentation.

I had already taken pictures before the ventilator.

Those had been updates.
Warnings I didn't know were warnings.
A slow visual record of decline I didn't understand while I was inside it.

This was different.

This was the first picture after.

The first one taken when I was stable enough to really look back.

And for the first time since I had come into the hospital, I was looking at survival instead of deterioration.

That was new.

I looked better than I had before they intubated me.

That was the first thing I saw.

Not healthy.
Not normal.

Better.

The distress was gone.

The panic in the face was gone.
The visible strain was gone.
The look of someone actively losing ground had lifted.

That part was better.

But "better" and "well" are not the same thing.

That was the second thing I saw.

I looked old.

Not older.

Old.

Not worn down.
Not tired.
Not sick in the familiar way.

Old in a way that felt abrupt.

Like I had skipped decades in a week.

Like something had accelerated inside me and dragged the surface with it.

That was the shock.

Not that I looked sick.

That I looked eighty.

It was in the face first.

The cheeks had fallen in.
The structure was sharper.
The softness was gone.

My face looked hollowed out.

Not thinner in the flattering way people talk about weight loss.

Reduced.

Like my body had burned through everything unnecessary and left only what it needed to keep going.

That was what survival looked like in the face.

Efficiency.

Nothing extra.
Nothing soft.
Nothing spared.

The grey hit harder than I expected.

Not because grey hair is dramatic.

Because it looked sudden.

Not gradual.
Not earned.
Not age arriving the way age is supposed to arrive.

It looked like it had happened overnight.

Like stress had surfaced all at once and settled into my hair and beard before I had even opened my eyes.

That was harder to process than it should have been.

It felt visible.

Not cosmetic.

Damage.

That was what unsettled me.

Not vanity.

Evidence.

The weight loss didn't hit me until the picture did.

I knew I was weaker.
I knew I was lighter.
I knew the bed and the tremor in my hands had already told me that much.

But the photo made it measurable.

Nearly thirty pounds gone.

Not abstractly.

Visibly.

That was when absence became real.

You can feel weak and still negotiate with it.

You can tell yourself weakness is temporary.
That it's the bed.
That it's the illness.
That it's the drugs.

The photo removes negotiation.

It makes loss visible.

And visible loss is harder to argue with.

My face took the worst of it.

That was where the shock landed.

Not the weight.
Not the beard.
Not even the grey.

The eyes.

They were the first thing I looked for.

And the first thing that felt wrong.

People say the eyes are the gateway to the soul.

In that picture, there was nothing in them I recognized.

That was the part that stopped me.

Not because they were dead.

Because they were absent.

Not empty.

Vacated.

I recognized my face.
I knew it was me.
There was no question about that.

But whatever usually lived behind the eyes had not fully made it back yet.

That was the part the camera caught before I had words for it.

I looked like me.

And I didn't.

That was the first true confrontation with what survival had cost.

Not in theory.
Not in numbers.
Not in charts.
Not in oxygen.

In the face.

That was what made it real.

Not that I had almost died.

That this was what surviving it looked like.

That was the first time survival became expensive enough to see.

And that changed something.

Until then, survival had still felt clinical.

A sequence.
A process.
A series of events I was still moving through.

The picture ended that.

It made survival personal.

Visible.

Irreversible.

That was not the face of someone who had simply been sick.

That was the face of someone who had been taken apart and returned.

And for the first time, looking back at myself through the camera, I understood both things at once:

I had survived long enough to become someone I recognized—

and someone I didn't.

PART III — THE RETURN

12. The Broken Machine

I had been breathing on my own for two days. No ventilator. No sedation. No restraints. Just me, the oxygen line, and a stubborn will to recover.

So when they asked if I wanted to try walking, I didn't hesitate.

"Yes," I rasped. Or maybe I just nodded. Either way, I meant it.

I was ready.

Until I wasn't.

The physical therapist came in with a clipboard, a gait belt, and the kind of quiet confidence that told me she had done this before. She spoke softly, like someone trying not to startle a wounded animal.

“Let’s try sitting up first,” she said. “Then we’ll go from there.”

She raised the bed and helped swing my legs over the side.

It should not have felt monumental.

But it did.

My feet hung over the edge of the mattress and I sat there trying to process the effort it had taken just to get upright. It felt like standing on the edge of a cliff, except I was still sitting down.

Then I looked at my legs.

They looked normal.

That was the first surprise.

No dramatic wasting. No skeletal collapse. No obvious sign that anything had changed. Pale maybe. Thinner maybe. But not shocking. Not at first glance.

They looked like my legs.

That was what made the next part worse.

I told them to move.

Nothing happened.

Not pain. Not resistance. Nothing.

I stared at them and tried again, harder this time, willing the signal downward the way you do without ever thinking about it. Tighten the muscle. Lift the leg. Move.

Nothing.

My brain sent the command. My body did not answer.

That was the first real shock.

Not weakness.

Disconnection.

It was not that my legs hurt too much to move. It was that they felt disconnected from the command entirely, like the signal had somewhere to go and simply stopped before it got there.

I remember staring at them in disbelief, trying again, then again, waiting for something automatic to happen.

Nothing.

The therapist watched my face more than my legs.

“It’s okay,” she said. “Muscle memory takes time.”

“No,” I whispered. “I should be able to…”

I stopped because I could hear how absurd it sounded the second it left my mouth.

Should.

As if surviving a ventilator came with guarantees.

My right leg twitched.

That was it.

One small twitch. Barely enough to count as movement. But it was enough to tell me the line was still intact.

I tried to lift my foot an inch off the bed.

It felt like trying to deadlift a car.

Not painful.

Impossible.

The effort it took to attempt something that small was humiliating. The kind of weakness that strips ego out of a person quickly.

She put a hand on my shoulder.

"We'll get there."

But I didn't feel reassured.

I felt afraid.

Not because I thought I was dying.

Because for the first time, I understood survival had not returned me intact.

I had walked into that hospital.

Now I couldn't lift my own leg.

That was the first real cost.

Not the ventilator. Not the sedation. Not the memory gap.

This.

The body that had survived no longer worked the way I expected it to.

That was harder to accept than almost dying.

The weakness was humbling.

The dependence was worse.

The urinal proved that quickly.

They handed it to me like it was routine. Because to them, it was.

To me, it was something else entirely.

Using it was not physically difficult.

It was mentally brutal.

No privacy. No dignity. No distance between need and dependence. Just a plastic jug, trembling hands, and the quiet understanding that even this now required help.

I hated asking for it.

I hated needing it more.

But the worst part was not the urinal.

It was soiling the bed.

That was the most humiliating moment of recovery.

No warning worth reacting to. No time to move. No control over the timing, the body, or the outcome.

Just the immediate realization of what had happened and the certainty that someone else was now going to have to clean it.

That was worse than the weakness.

Worse than the shaking.

Worse than the helplessness.

Humiliation has a different weight when you are fully awake for it.

The nurse came in with gloves, clean sheets, and practiced calm.

She did not flinch.

She did not hesitate.

She changed the bedding, cleaned me up, and moved through it with the kind of professionalism that should have made it easier.

It didn't.

I turned my face toward the wall.

I could not look at her.

She told me not to be embarrassed.

That it happens all the time.

I believed her.

It did not matter.

The loss of privacy was humiliating.

The loss of control was worse.

And beneath both of them was the harder truth:

I was dependent.

Not temporarily inconvenienced.

Dependent.

Every movement required help.
Every need had to be asked for.
Every basic function required either assistance, permission, or both.

I had spent my life being useful. Carrying weight. Solving problems. Providing for everyone around me.

Now I needed help to sit up, help to stand, help to piss, help to clean myself, help to eat.

That landed harder than the weakness.

Weakness can be trained back.

Dependence is something else.

That was the first real humiliation of surviving.

By the time they sat me up again that afternoon, I understood what they were actually asking me to do.

This was not standing.

This was proof.

The blood shifted the second I sat upright.

Exhaustion hit first.

Not dizziness. Not panic. Exhaustion.

Immediate and overwhelming, like simply being vertical had tripled the energy demand.

My body started sweating. My arms trembled. My heart began working harder than the movement justified.

The therapist tightened the belt around my waist and slid her arm behind my back.

"Don't lock your knees," she said. "Just breathe."

I nodded.

She counted.

"Three. Two. One."

And I stood.

Barely.

Everything shook.

My knees buckled immediately. My ankles felt unstable. My legs held just enough weight to keep me upright and not one ounce more.

It wasn't pain.

It was mechanical failure.

My body did not trust itself.

That was what standing felt like.

Not pain. Not triumph.

A broken machine trying to remember how to function.

I gripped the walker hard enough to hurt my hands.

My legs were shaky, weak, and disconnected all at once—like my brain was sending commands through damaged wiring and hoping something at the other end still worked.

I was upright.

But only technically.

Then I looked down.

My feet were on the floor.

That hit first.

Relief.

Then disbelief.

They were holding me.

Barely. Unsteadily. Imperfectly.

But they were holding.

Not the bed.

Not the rails.

Not the restraints.

The floor.

That was the moment it landed.

Not that I had stood.

What it had cost to do it.

That was why I cried.

Not because I was standing.

Because I had almost lost the ability to.

Because surviving had cost more than breath.

Because this was the first moment I understood survival had kept me alive—but it had not spared me.

The therapist kept one hand on my back.

"We'll try a step tomorrow," she said.

I didn't answer.

I just cried.

13. Floor Life

The room was too quiet.

No ventilator hum. No constant pulse ox beeping. No nurse hovering within arm's reach, monitoring every breath.

Just a window. A bed. A mounted TV I didn't bother turning on. And a wall-mounted dry-erase board that read: Goal for Today: Eat. Sit. Try to stand.

I stared at it longer than I meant to.

They wheeled me in that morning — post-ICU, post-second scare. The handoff was polite, professional. But I saw it in their faces: I wasn't critical anymore. I was stable.

Which meant… I was lower priority now.

It wasn't neglect. It was reality.

ICU had a 1:1 or 1:2 nurse-patient ratio. But here, on the floor, nurses had five or six patients.

Sometimes more. The CNA — or maybe she was a CMA, I couldn't tell — was the one who took vitals. Brought urinals. Answered the call button when she could.

And they were kind. Don't get me wrong.

But it was different.

In ICU, I was a crisis.

Here, I was recovery.

And recovery moved slow.

Still on high-flow oxygen — 15 liters blasting into my nose. Still needing help to use the urinal. Still couldn't walk on my own. My legs felt like sandbags, uncooperative and distant. I had to be hoisted, pivoted, coached.

But I wasn't intubated.

I wasn't dying.

So now I waited.

For therapy.

For meals.

For vitals.

For my next breath, sometimes.

No one could visit. Still full COVID protocol. No family allowed. No friendly faces walking in with flowers or jokes or just a warm hand on mine.

But I had my phone.

And it buzzed constantly.

Thirty-nine unread texts.

Amber. Lauren. Friends. Coworkers I hadn't seen in months.

People had been watching from the outside. Praying. Worrying. Wondering if I'd make it.

I read every message twice. Sometimes three times. Some were simple — "You got this" or "Thinking of you." Others were walls of love and fear and everything in between.

I tried to respond. Not with full thoughts — I wasn't there yet — but with short replies. Emojis. "Still here." "Thanks." "Breathing."

It took everything I had.

Sometimes I'd write the same word three times before I spelled it right.

But I was answering.

That counted for something.

A nurse came in mid-morning. Young. Efficient. A little rushed.

She checked the oxygen machine. Took vitals. Asked if I wanted breakfast.

I said no.

I just wanted water.

She nodded, wrote something on the dry-erase board, and left.

The quiet returned.

I stared at the board again.

“Eat. Sit. Try to stand.”

The smallest goals in the world.

And yet, somehow, they looked like Everest.

Time didn’t pass here.

It stalled.

Then repeated itself.

Each hour was a copy of the one before: A knock. A blood pressure cuff. A temperature strip tucked under my tongue. A plastic cup of pills I couldn’t name. A tray of food I couldn’t eat. The same questions: “Pain?” “Nausea?” “Did you go today?”

I stopped answering unless they looked me in the eye.

The nurse came and went like a ghost. Quiet, professional, always carrying a tablet. She spoke in checkboxes: “How’s your pain scale?” “Any shortness of breath?” “Any bowel movements?”

But it was the CNA who knew me.

Her name escaped me.

She wheeled the vitals cart. Changed my sheets when they were damp. Wiped me off with warm washcloths and said, “Ain’t nobody dignified in a hospital, baby — only alive.” She didn’t rush. Didn’t flinch. She called me sugar and boss and sweetheart, and she meant every one of them.

When my call button went unanswered for 20 minutes, she was the one who found me shaking, the oxygen line knocked loose again. Not all the way off — just enough to make me dizzy. She fixed it without fuss. Didn’t even tell the nurse. “I got you,” she whispered, tucking the line tight against my ear.

That was floor life.

Not emergencies.

Just little losses.

Like time. Like control. Like warmth.

PT showed up that afternoon — two of them this time, a man and a woman. Clipboards, gait belt, masks. They wanted me to try walking again. I nodded like I had a choice.

I sat up. Swung my legs down. Felt the tremble in my thighs as they dangled.

They strapped the belt around my waist and one stood behind me.

“On three.”

“One…”

“Two…”

“Three…”

I stood.

Sort of.

They kept me upright, one on each side. My knees didn't buckle, but they felt like they wanted to.

We took one step.

Then another.

Then I sat again — not because I chose to, but because I couldn't stay up.

I felt sweat rolling down my back like I'd just finished a marathon.

They called it a win.

And it was.

But it didn't feel like one.

Not yet.

14. Home Oxygen

Discharge was not the finish line.

It was the handoff.

That was the first thing I understood when they started talking about sending me home.

Nobody used language dramatic enough to say it that way, but that was the truth underneath all of it.

Discharge was not recovery.
It was transfer.

The hospital had done what it was built to do.

It had kept me alive.
Stabilized me.

Pulled me through the first emergency.
Gotten me to the point where I no longer needed a ventilator, no longer needed constant intervention, no longer needed a room full of machines to do the work my body could not.

That did not mean I was well.

It meant I was stable enough to leave.

There is a difference between being healed and being discharged.

I understood that before I ever got in the car.

Leaving the hospital felt like a victory, but not in the clean way people imagine survival.

There was no cinematic feeling to it.
No moment where everything suddenly felt behind me.
No clean emotional release.

I had won something, yes.

But what I had won was permission to continue recovering somewhere else.

That was all.

It was not triumph.

It was transition.

I left the hospital alive, but what left with me was not the version of me that had gone in.

What came home was a shell.

Not in the dramatic sense.

In the clinical one.

I was upright.
Breathing.
Talking.
Discharged.

But hollowed out.

There is no cleaner way to say it.

The hospital had saved my life, but it had not returned me to it.

The drive home felt fragile.

I do not remember much of the conversation, if there was any at all.

I assume Amber and I talked.

I'm sure we did.

But memory does not hold the words.

Only the feeling.

It was not silence exactly.

It was fragility.

The kind that makes conversation feel secondary to what is sitting in the car with you.

Amber told me later there was a moment before the ride home when she did not recognize me.

Not because she did not know it was me.

Because the man coming out of the hospital did not match the husband she had watched walk into it.

The weight was gone.

The color was wrong.

My face was hollowed out.

My hair and beard had gone gray in a way that looked sudden, almost violent.

I was moving slowly, carefully, oxygen attached, every step looking borrowed.

For a second, she had to put me together.

Face.

Voice.

Eyes.

Husband.

That is what survival had done before I ever saw myself clearly at home.

It made the person who loved me most have to look twice.

I do not blame her for that.

I understand it.

I barely recognized myself either.

She was seeing me outside the hospital for the first time.

Not through a doorway.
Not under fluorescent light.
Not framed by monitors and tubing and the machinery that had explained away some of what I looked like.

She was seeing me in daylight.

In normal clothes.
In motion.
Leaving.

And I know now she was trying to reconcile two things at once:

that I was coming home,
and what home was coming home with.

That ride was not relief.

It was inventory.

At some point in the car, Amber took a selfie of us.

I remember thinking I smiled for it.

Not a big smile.

Just enough to say I was there.

Alive.

Coming home.

Later, when I looked at the picture, it did not even look like I had tried.

That was one of the strangest parts of recovery. Inside my own head, I still thought I was participating more than I was. I thought effort showed. I thought life showed. I thought relief showed.

The picture told a different story.

Amber was beside me, smiling because she had me in the car and not in a hospital bed. I was there beside her, but the face in that photo looked distant. Hollow. Exhausted. Barely present.

Not unhappy.

Not expressionless exactly.

Just emptied out in a way I had not fully understood until I saw it.

I had thought I was smiling.

The camera said otherwise.

That photo showed me something my body had been trying to tell me all along:

I was home, but I was still only partially back.

The first walk into my own house on oxygen was the real transition.

That was the moment it became undeniable.

I was not walking into my own home under my own power.

Not fully.

I did not have a choice.

Without the oxygen, I was not making that walk.

That matters.

There is something brutally clarifying about dragging oxygen tubing through your own front door.

Hospitals normalize dependency because everything in them is built around it.

Home does not.

At home, dependency looks unnatural immediately.

There was no staff.
No rails.

No monitors.
No context to soften what it meant.

Just me.
My house.
And thirty feet of oxygen tubing following me in like a leash.

That was the moment discharge became real.

Not in the paperwork.

In the tubing.

Home was familiar.
Comforting.
Immediate relief in the emotional sense.

It smelled right.
It felt right.
It was mine again.

That mattered.

But familiarity and recovery are not the same thing.

Home comfort can hide a lot for about ten minutes.

Then reality catches up.

The oxygen tubing made sure of that.

At first, it felt like being tethered to a boat anchor.

Thirty feet of line dragging behind me through the house.
Catching on corners.
Looping under furniture.
Brushing against walls.
Following me into every room.

It announced itself constantly.

Every movement had a tail.

Every step had a reminder.

Every shift in the house carried evidence that I was not moving freely.

That was the first humiliation of being home.

Not pain.

Dependence made visible.

After a few days, it became normal enough to stop thinking about.

At first, it felt like being tethered to the proof that I was not okay.

That was harder.

The first night home was better than I expected.

I slept propped up on two pillows, still on oxygen, still exhausted enough that sleep came quickly.

That part surprised me.

Hospital sleep is survival sleep.
Interrupted.
Measured.
Never fully yours.

Home sleep was different.

Not better because I was healthier.

Better because I was home.

That distinction mattered.

Home did not make me stronger.

It just made rest feel like rest again.

That was enough for one night.

The next morning was the first real confrontation.

The shower.

That was the moment recovery became measurable.

Not in oxygen numbers.
Not in discharge instructions.
Not in medication.

In a shower.

The water was the first mercy.

It was the first real shower I had taken in nearly a month.

The first time I had felt clean.
Actually clean.
Not wiped down.
Not managed.
Not medically maintained.

Clean.

That mattered more than I expected.

The water felt restorative in a way almost nothing else had.

It felt human.

It felt familiar.

It felt like the first normal thing I had done in weeks.

And for about thirty seconds, it felt wonderful.

Then the cost showed up.

The shower chair was not optional.

It was mandatory.

That mattered immediately.

Not because sitting in the shower was symbolic.

Because it was necessary.

I did not have enough in me to stand through it.

That was not theory.
Not caution.
Not overcorrection.

It was math.

Standing long enough to shower would have cost more than I had.

So I sat.

And sitting there, under hot water, in my own shower, breathing through oxygen tubing, was the first brutally honest measure of how far from normal I still was.

The heat took more out of me than I expected.

The humidity made everything harder.

Breathing in damp air felt heavy.
Dense.
Resistant.

The air itself felt like work.

That was the first time I realized even breathing had conditions now.

I had to think about it.

In through the nose.
Out through the mouth.
Slow.
Measured.
Controlled.

Even showering required strategy.

That changes how you understand weakness.

The water felt incredible.

That may have made it worse.

Because it reminded me exactly what normal used to feel like.

The comfort was familiar.

The effort was not.

That contrast made the truth unavoidable.

I was home.

I was not back.

By the time I finished, I had nothing left.

Not tired.

Spent.

There is a difference.

Tired implies more is available after rest.

Spent means the tank is empty now.

That was what the shower cost.

Everything.

Amber helped me dry off.
Helped me get dressed.
Helped me get into pajamas.

That detail matters.

Not because it was dramatic.

Because it was ordinary in a way that should never have been necessary.

Then I went straight to bed.

Not later.
Not after breakfast.
Not after sitting for a while.

Immediately.

That was the first real proof that discharge had not meant recovery.

A shower had taken every ounce of strength I had.

The hospital had hidden some of that.

Hospitals absorb weakness.
They are built for it.

Staff compensates.
Structure compensates.
The room compensates.

Home does not.

At home, the body is exposed.

There are no buffers.
No systems absorbing the deficit.
No staff stepping in before the cost becomes obvious.

At home, every ordinary task becomes a diagnostic test.

The shower was the first one.

And it was brutally honest.

That was what home exposed that the hospital could not.

Not just that I was weak.

That my body was still mostly a vessel.

And a weak one.

Amber became everything the hospital no longer was.

She was my wife.

She was also my nurse.
My support staff.
My safety net.
The one compensating for what my body still could not do.

She carried more of that burden than I could have reasonably asked anyone to carry.

And she did it anyway.

She was my rock.

There is no cleaner way to say it.

The hospital had kept me alive.

Amber carried me through what came next.

Home was comforting.

It was also humbling.

It put the truth in scale quickly.

I was alive.
I was home.
I was still far from well.

And the first shower made that impossible to misunderstand.

The hospital had kept me breathing.

The first shower at home taught me how far I still was from living.

15. The Stairs

The stairs became a problem the moment physical therapy decided they mattered.

Until then, recovery at home had stayed small.

Standing.
Walking across the room.
Getting from the chair to the bathroom.
Learning how to move through the day without spending everything too early.

That was enough at first.

For the first week, those were the victories.

Measured.
Manageable.
Contained.

Then physical therapy decided it was time to move the line.

They had mentioned the stairs a day or two before.

Not casually.

Like a warning.

Something to prepare for.

Not because there was something upstairs I needed.

There wasn't.

That was the point.

Nothing upstairs was urgent.

No medication.
No necessity.
No emergency.

The stairs mattered because they existed.

Because normal life included them.

Because if I could not climb them, then some part of normal still belonged to the house and not to me.

That was the real test.

The stairs were not practical.

They were symbolic.

And because of that, they mattered more.

By then the walker had already become part of the routine.

Not an insult.

Not a humiliation.

Just a tool.

By that point, pride had already lost enough battles to stop making everything personal.

The walker did what it was supposed to do.

It stabilized me.
Bought me margin.
Gave me enough support to move without spending unnecessary energy trying to prove I didn't need help.

That mattered.

The walker wasn't the problem.

The stairs were.

Physical therapy had me walk to them first.

That alone took effort.

Not enough to matter in normal life.
Enough to matter in mine.

The walker got me there.

Then the therapist told me to leave it.

Just hold the railing.

They'd be behind me if I needed help.

That was the moment the stairs changed shape.

Until then, they had just been part of the house.

A structure.
A feature.
A staircase.

Then they became work.

I remember the first few steps clearly because of how little it took.

Two.
Maybe three.
Possibly four.

That was enough.

Done.

Spent.

That was the first lesson.

Not halfway.
Not the full flight.

Three steps.

That was what my lungs had for me.

The legs held longer than the lungs did.

That surprised me.

The weakness was there, but it was not what failed first.

My legs could still push.

My lungs could not support what they were being asked to do.

That was the problem.

By the third step, I had already spent the reserve.

That was what stairs exposed better than anything else in the house.

Not whether I could move.

Whether I could sustain it.

The climb itself was hard.

The cost was harder.

Because the steps up were only half the work.

Then I had to come back down.

Two to four steps back to the floor.
Back to the walker.
Back across the room.
Back to the chair.

And by then I was out of breath enough to feel the full bill come due.

That was the part that changed how I understood effort.

The body lies on the way up.

That was the lesson.

Your brain tells you that you're doing fine.
That you're moving.
That you're making progress.
That the work is happening and the body is responding.

Then the lungs answer.

And they are always more honest.

That was the reality of the stairs.

My brain said progress.

My lungs said not yet.

That was the first true argument between effort and capacity.

And the lungs won every time.

The first attempt was discouraging.

Not because I failed.

Because of how little it took to empty me.

Three steps should not feel like a fight.

Three steps should not burn through every reserve you have.

Three steps should not send you back to a chair trying to recover oxygen like you had just finished something far more serious than a staircase.

But that was the truth of it.

And truth is rarely flattering.

By the time I got back to the chair, I was done.

Not metaphorically.

Done.

It took about ten minutes for my oxygen saturation to recover enough for PT to even consider leaving.

That mattered.

Not because of the number.

Because of what it meant.

The work had ended.
The cost had not.

That was the lesson.

Stairs kept taking from you long after you stopped moving.

That was what made them different.

The shower emptied the tank.

The stairs kept charging interest.

That was the first thing in the house that truly felt bigger than me.

Physical therapy pushed.

That was their job.

Not recklessly.
Not carelessly.

But consistently.

Every other day they moved the line.

That was the rhythm.

Push.
Recover.
Repeat.

They did not let discouragement become the stopping point.

That mattered.

Because the stairs became the first real measuring stick of progress.

Not the shower.
Not the walker.
Not the oxygen tubing.

The stairs.

They became the yardstick.

The one fixed thing in the house that did not care how I felt.

The stairs did not care if I was tired.
Did not care if I was frustrated.
Did not care if I thought I was improving.

They answered only one question:

Can you do more today than yesterday?

That was the metric.

And because of that, the stairs stopped being part of the house.

They became rehab.

That was the shift.

Home stopped being just home the moment the staircase became a scoreboard.

At first, they humbled me.

Then they irritated me.

Then they became personal.

Not because I needed what was upstairs.

Because they were there.

And because they had become the clearest measure of whether I was actually coming back.

They became Everest.

Not all at once.

But quickly.

One section.
Then one landing.
Then more.

Every few days the summit moved a little closer.

Every few days the body gave a little more back.

And every step cost something.

Oxygen.
Strength.
Recovery.
Focus.
Will.

Everything was spent in pieces.

That was the trade.

The full flight did not come quickly.

It took about a month.

A month of practice.
A month of repetition.
A month of climbing the same stretch of stairs until they stopped being a barrier and started becoming movement again.

That was the work.

Not dramatic.
Not cinematic.

Just repetitive enough to matter.

By the time I reached the top, the stairs had stopped being part of the house.

They had become the work.

16. The First Drive

I do not remember exactly where I went the first time I drove again.

That feels appropriate.

The destination was never the point.

Leaving was.

It had been at least three weeks since I got home.

Long enough to be moving better.
Long enough to think I should try.
Not long enough to be normal.

I was still on oxygen.

Two liters.

That mattered before I ever turned the key.

The first challenge was not driving.

It was getting into the car.

That was the first reality check.

The Camry helped.

It sat low enough to the ground that getting in was easier than it would have been in anything taller.

That mattered more than I expected.

The problem was not the car.

The problem was everything required before I was even in it.

Opening the door.
Managing the oxygen tank.
Handling the tubing.
Getting settled without spending too much energy before I had even started the engine.

That was the part no one thinks about.

The logistics of weakness.

Even simple movements become layered when you have to do them while tethered to what is keeping you upright.

It took more out of me than it should have.

That was becoming familiar.

By then, everything did.

The oxygen in the car felt normal enough to function.

Not normal enough to ignore.

That distinction mattered.

It was usable.

It worked.

But it was still visible.

Still obvious.

Still one more thing to make me self-conscious in a way I had never had to consider before.

Not because anyone was looking.

Because I knew it was there.

That changes the experience.

You stop moving through the world anonymously when your recovery is visible.

That was new.

Getting behind the wheel felt familiar.

That part came back faster than I expected.

Muscle memory took over quickly.

That was the surprising part.

Driving is like riding a bike.

You do not forget how to do it.

The mechanics were still there.

Hands on the wheel.
Foot on the pedal.
Eyes moving where they were supposed to move.

The body remembered.

That was never the problem.

The problem was everything layered on top of it.

Driving felt familiar.

It did not feel normal.

That distinction mattered.

The physical act came back quickly.

The mental load did not.

That was the real surprise.

Physically, driving was manageable.

Mentally, it was exhausting.

That was the cost.

The movement of traffic.
The speed of everything.
The constant motion in the periphery.
Cars passing.
Lights shifting.
Movement from every direction.

My brain had a hard time keeping up with all of it.

That was the first thing I noticed.

Not fear.

Overload.

The world moved faster than I did.

That was the problem.

Not physically.

Mentally.

My mind was trying to process traffic at the speed it used to.
My body was present.
My reflexes were functional.
But the part of me sorting and prioritizing all of it felt delayed.

Not dangerously.

But noticeably.

Enough to know I was not operating at full speed yet.

That made driving different.

Not because I could not do it.

Because I could feel how much harder my brain was working to do something that used to happen automatically.

That was the real fatigue.

The body tolerated the drive.

The mind paid for it.

That was the cost.

Driving did not empty me physically the way the shower had.
It did not take from my legs the way the stairs had.

It took from my mind.

That was different.

And harder to measure.

Physical weakness is visible.
Mental fatigue is quieter.

It just makes everything feel louder than it should.

That was driving in those first weeks.

A continuous battle of the senses.

Too much movement.
Too much input.
Too much to track all at once.

It took a few weeks before driving started to feel normal again.

Until then, every drive was work.

Not because I was afraid.

Because I was processing.

That was the difference.

Being alone was the point.

More than the destination.
More than the errand.
More than wherever I was technically going.

Leaving the house without someone helping me mattered.

That was the victory.

Not freedom.

Independence.

Even borrowed.

That distinction mattered too.

It did not feel like freedom.

Not fully.

It felt like borrowed independence.

Enough to leave.
Enough to function.
Enough to remember what autonomy felt like.

Not enough to pretend I had it all back.

That was the truth of it.

The oxygen made sure of that.

The fatigue made sure of that.

The self-consciousness made sure of that.

I could leave the house.

I just could not leave the reality of what had happened behind with it.

Part of me knew I was pushing early.

Not recklessly.

But early.

The body could tolerate more than the brain could process.

That was the mismatch.

And it took time to close.

The first drive left me hopeful.

And frustrated.

Hopeful because I could feel pieces of normal returning.

Frustrated because I could also feel how incomplete that return still was.

That was the tension in early recovery.

Everything was coming back.

Just not all at once.

Driving proved I could leave the house.

It did not prove I had returned to my life.

17. The First Public Room

The first public room I walked into after the hospital was a restaurant.

Not a clinic.
Not a waiting room.
Not a follow-up appointment where weakness was expected and oxygen made sense.

A restaurant.

We went to Habaneros for my birthday on September 21st.

Three weeks after discharge.

That mattered.

Not because it was dramatic.

Because three weeks earlier, there was no guarantee I would make it to my next birthday at all.

That changed what a birthday meant.

The first public room was not about being seen.

It was about being there.

That was the difference.

I was still on oxygen.

At least two liters.

That part was not optional.

By then it was simply part of the logistics.

Bring the tank.
Manage the tubing.

Make sure there was enough to get there, get in, sit down, and get home.

That had already become routine enough to stop feeling dramatic.

Not normal.

Routine.

There is a difference.

Walking into the restaurant felt more normal than it had any right to.

That surprised me.

I did not walk in thinking about the oxygen.
I did not walk in thinking about what I looked like.
I did not walk in wondering who would stare.

I did not think about any of that.

It was my birthday.

I was paying attention to my family.

That was it.

That was the first real surprise of being back in public.

No one cared.

No one stared.
No one paused.
No one paid attention to the oxygen.
No one watched me walk in.
No one looked twice.

That was not offensive.

It was comforting.

There is something deeply stabilizing about learning the world did not stop for what happened to you.

The world keeps moving.

Most people are too occupied with their own lives to inventory yours.

That is not cruelty.

It is relief.

I had spent weeks inside a version of life where everything narrowed down to breath, oxygen, effort, recovery, progress, and what my body could or could not do.

The hospital makes everything about survival.

Recovery makes everything about survival.

Public life does not.

That was the lesson.

To everyone else, it was just dinner.

That was more comforting than I expected it to be.

It meant I could be in the room without the room becoming about me.

That mattered.

The oxygen came off when I sat down.

That mattered too.

Not medically for long.
Not symbolically in some dramatic way.

Practically.

I did not want to sit there with oxygen blowing across my face while I ate.

Taking it off for dinner felt like a small piece of normal returning.

Not because it meant I did not need it.

Because it let me ignore it for a little while.

That was enough.

The walk in and out was still work.

By then it was better.

Not easy.
Not normal.

But better.

Three weeks home had already moved the line enough that the walk from the car to the table no longer felt like an event.

It still cost something.

Just not everything.

That mattered.

The dinner itself felt celebratory in more ways than one.

It was my birthday.

That was enough by itself.

But it was also something else.

I had made it to the next one.

That changed the room.

You do not sit through a birthday dinner the same way after almost missing the date entirely.

The food mattered more.
The conversation mattered more.
The fact of being there mattered more.

And beyond that, I had made it out of the hospital.

That was still sitting at the table too.

No one had to say it out loud.

It was there anyway.

That made the dinner feel larger than dinner.

Not dramatic.

Earned.

By then I could eat normally again.

That mattered too.

Not because the food was remarkable.

Because I could enjoy it.

No swallowing exercises.
No thickened liquids.
No measuring effort against every bite.

Just dinner.

That had become enough to feel like progress.

My parents came.

That is the part that stayed with me most.

It was good to see them.

That alone would have been enough.

But what stayed was not just that they were there.

It was how my father walked in.

He came through the door carrying the same kind of portable oxygen tank I had.

Small.
Compact.
Familiar.

That was the first thing I noticed.

Then I noticed the rest.

He was pale.

More than he should have been.

I had my pulse oximeter with me.

I told him to sit down and check his oxygen.

His sats were in the 70s.

That was after just walking in.

Peak exertion had dropped him into the 70s.

Once he sat for a few minutes, they climbed back into the low 90s.

At the time, it registered as concerning.

Looking back, it feels obvious.

No wonder he was gone four months later.

That was the part of that dinner I did not understand yet.

At the time, it was just data.
Just another oxygen number.
Just another moment in a season where I had become conditioned to monitor breath as a measure of what came next.

Now it reads differently.

Now it feels like foreshadowing.

At the time, it was just my birthday dinner.

That is what memory does.

It lets moments remain ordinary until time makes them heavier.

What stayed with me most about that room was not being seen.

It was being ignored.

And I mean that in the best possible way.

No one cared.

No one looked.
No one stared.
No one made the room about what had happened to me.

The world had not stopped for what happened to me.

My family had.

And that was enough.

18. The First Day Back

I did not go back to work when I came home.

Not really.

I maintained it.

That was different.

For the first two months after discharge, work existed in the narrowest form possible.

Phone calls.
Check-ins.
Maintenance.

I worked from the house because that was all I could do.

No in-person meetings.
No clinic visits.
No customer stops.
No travel.
No overnight stays.

Nothing that resembled the version of work I had spent years building my life around.

That part stopped.

And that mattered more than I expected.

At first, the calls were practical.

Reassurance.
Maintenance.
Presence.

I was not working in the way I had worked before.

I was keeping the machine warm.

That was the job.

Let customers know I was alive.
Let them know I was still there.
Let them know if they needed something, they could call me.
Let them know I would be back when I could.

That was the extent of it.

No clinic.
No in-person support.
No field work.

Just enough presence to prevent absence from becoming replacement.

That was the reality of work in recovery.

Not return.

Maintenance.

And even that had limits.

The first few weeks, a couple of hours was enough to empty me.

Not physically.

Mentally.

That was the part recovery had not prepared me for.

The body had made itself obvious.

The brain was quieter.

And in some ways, worse.

COVID brain was real.

Still is.

That was the first place work exposed what recovery had hidden.

The physical deficits were easy to track.

The mental ones were harder.

I could tell when my body was tired.

The brain was different.

It just stopped cooperating.

Focus would collapse first.
Then recall.
Then continuity.

I would lose my train of thought in the middle of speaking.
Know what I meant.
Know where I was going.
And still need a second for my brain to catch up to my mouth.

That part never fully left.

It still hasn't.

I still preface serious conversations with the same sentence:

I have COVID brain. Bear with me.

Especially with new customers.

Especially when precision matters.

That became the new accommodation.

Not oxygen.
Not a walker.
Not visible recovery.

A processing delay.

That was harder to explain because it looked like nothing.

Working from home was useful.

But only in the sense that maintenance is useful.

It kept things from breaking.

It did not build anything.

It was enough to preserve continuity.
Enough to keep customers from drifting.
Enough to keep income from collapsing while I caught up.

But it was not work in the way I had known it.

Not before.

Before COVID, work had been central.

Not just income.

Identity.

Routine.
Purpose.
Motion.
Validation.
Responsibility.

It was not just what I did.

It had become what I was.

That was the real shift recovery exposed.

By the time I was well enough to think clearly, work no longer sat in the same place.

It still mattered.

It paid the bills.

That part was unchanged.

But it was no longer the axis everything else rotated around.

That changed permanently.

Work was still necessary.

It was no longer the point.

That was the first real reordering.

And I knew it before I ever went back.

November 5th became the line.

Not because anything dramatic happened that day.

Because it was the first day I no longer needed home oxygen.

That was the threshold.

That was the first real marker that the next phase could begin.

No oxygen meant mobility.
Mobility meant range.
Range meant I could go back in person.

That made November 5th the natural line.

Not healed.

Just clear enough to re-enter.

The first clinic I went back to was RGG Cardiology in Mobile.

That felt right.

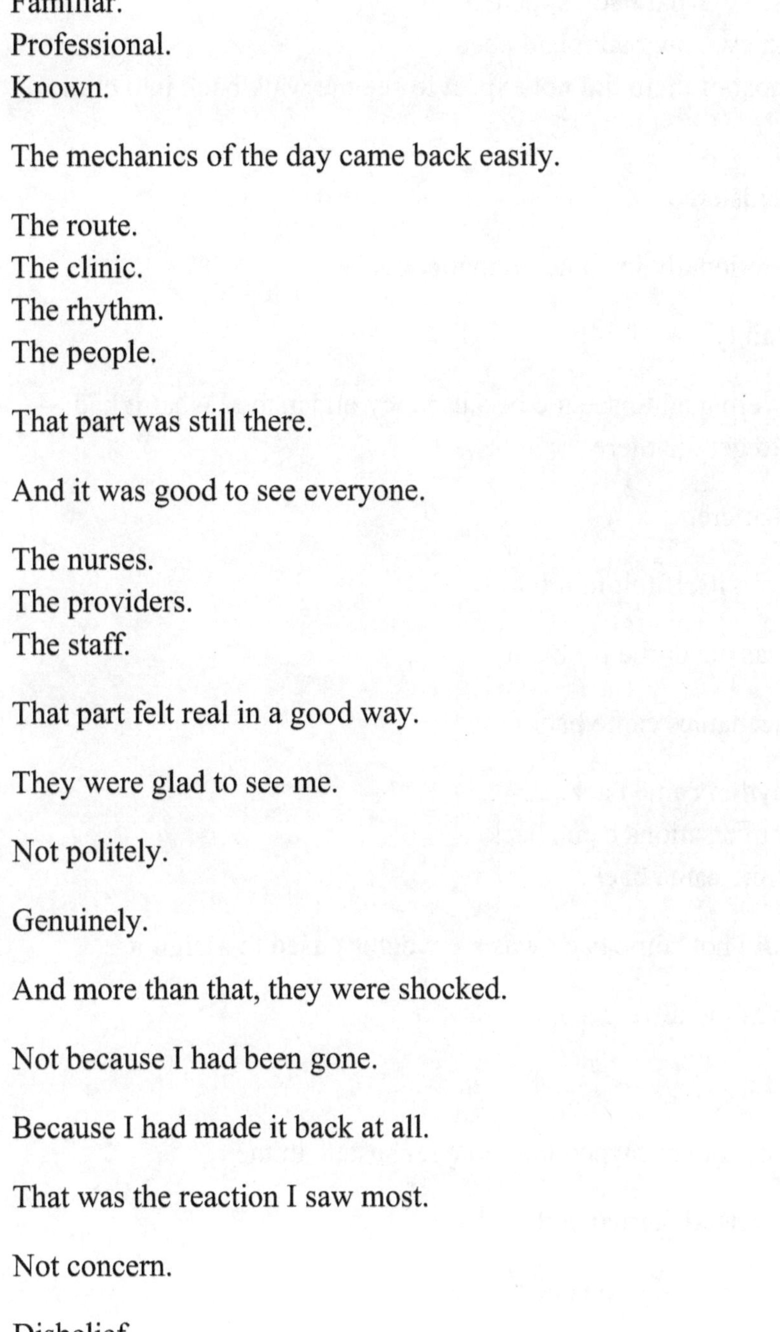

Familiar.
Professional.
Known.

The mechanics of the day came back easily.

The route.
The clinic.
The rhythm.
The people.

That part was still there.

And it was good to see everyone.

The nurses.
The providers.
The staff.

That part felt real in a good way.

They were glad to see me.

Not politely.

Genuinely.

And more than that, they were shocked.

Not because I had been gone.

Because I had made it back at all.

That was the reaction I saw most.

Not concern.

Disbelief.

They knew what had happened.
They knew how bad it had been.
And most of them did not expect to see me walk back into clinic again.

That registered.

Not emotionally in some dramatic way.

Just plainly.

They were glad to see me because they understood what it had taken to get me there.

That mattered.

The work itself felt familiar.

That was never the problem.

The mechanics came back.

The rhythm came back.
The conversations came back.
The clinic came back.

What did not come back was the weight I used to assign it.

That was the difference.

Work fit.

It just no longer owned the same real estate in me.

That changed permanently.

It was still good to be back.

It was good to see customers.
Good to reconnect.
Good to step back into something recognizable.

But it no longer held priority over the things it used to displace.

That part was over.

No more staying out of town.
No more missing family functions.
No more missing dinners because work ran long.
No more treating home like where I landed between obligations.

I made sure I was home at night.

That changed first.
And it stayed changed.

That was the line recovery drew through the rest of my life.

Work still mattered.

It just no longer outranked the people I nearly left behind.

That was the correction.

And once you see that clearly, you cannot unsee it.

Going back was necessary.

It was also disappointing.

And clarifying.

Necessary because income still mattered.
Disappointing because work no longer meant what it used to.
Clarifying because that loss of meaning was not loss at all.

It was correction.

That was what work exposed that recovery had hidden.

Not just fatigue.
Not just cognitive cost.
Not just the mental drag that still lingers.

It exposed what work had actually cost me long before COVID ever did.

Time.
Presence.
Dinners.
Nights at home.
Family.
Marriage.
Attention.
Life.

COVID did not create that truth.

It just removed enough noise to make it obvious.

Work had become what I did to pay my bills.

That was all.

Necessary.
Useful.
Important.

But no longer central.

I went back to work because I needed income.

I did not go back because I still believed work was the point.

19. COVID Brain

The first part of recovery was visible.

Oxygen.
Weakness.
Weight loss.
The walker.
The stairs.
The fatigue.

Those things were measurable.

People could see them.
I could see them.
They had shape.
They had evidence.

COVID brain was different.

That was the first part of recovery that looked like nothing and changed everything.

I knew something was off before I ever went back into the field.

There had already been moments at home where my thoughts simply vanished.

Not gradually.
Not like distraction.
Not normal forgetfulness.

Gone.

I would be in the middle of a thought, a sentence, a conversation, and then nothing.

Blank.

Not confusion.

Absence.

That was the first sign.

It was not dramatic from the outside.

From the inside, it was unmistakable.

That was what made it different.

This was not being tired.
Not being distracted.
Not forgetting where I put my keys.

This was a clear interruption in processing.

A visible break in continuity.

The thought was there.
Then it wasn't.

That is not something you confuse with normal.

That was the distinction.

And it was the first part of recovery that scared me more than the physical damage had.

The body had made sense.

The body was mechanical.

Weakness was frustrating, but understandable.

Lungs recover.
Muscles rebuild.
Endurance returns.

Slowly.
Imperfectly.
But predictably.

The brain was different.

The brain felt unreliable.

That was worse.

COVID brain was harder to define than the physical deficits, but easier to feel.

Sometimes it felt like delay.

Sometimes it felt like static.

Sometimes it felt like someone had simply pulled the plug on the middle of a thought and left me standing there trying to recover what had just disappeared.

That was the experience.

I could be in the middle of a sentence and feel my mind go blank in real time.

Not searching.

Blank.

That distinction matters.

Searching is normal.

Blank is different.

Blank is the sensation of knowing something should still be there and feeling the space where it used to be.

That was COVID brain.

And in real time, it was always the same sequence.

Pause.
Panic.
Embarrassment.
Apology.

That became the rhythm.

The pause long enough to feel it.
The panic when I realized the thought was gone.
The embarrassment when the silence became visible.
Then the apology while I tried to stitch together what had just disappeared in front of someone else.

That was the real cost.

Not forgetting.

Performing the gap.

That was worse.

And the more technical the conversation became, the more likely it was to happen.

That was what made work the clearest place to measure it.

The more precision required, the easier it was to lose the thread.

Small talk could survive a pause.

Technical conversation exposed every delay.

That was where COVID brain showed itself most clearly.

Not in ordinary conversation.

In specificity.

That was where I had always been sharpest.

That was what made it personal.

I had spent years making a living on precision.
Knowing what to say.
Knowing when to say it.
Knowing when to answer.
Knowing when not to.
And when I did not know, I knew exactly how to say that too.

My standard answer had always been simple:

I don't know, but I'll find out and get back to you this afternoon.

That had always been enough.

It was not the lack of answers that rattled me.

It was losing access to the thought in the first place.

That was different.

And harder.

That was the first time I felt less sharp than the version of myself I trusted.

That lands differently than physical weakness.

Physical weakness is humbling.

Mental hesitation is destabilizing.

That was the difference.

I compensated the way any good sales rep does.

I set the expectation before the problem arrived.

That became the strategy.

I started prefacing serious conversations the same way every time.

I have COVID brain. Bear with me.

Then I would laugh.

Make it light.
Make it easier.
Make it survivable.

Humor had always been part of how I worked.

That part came in handy.

I had always been a comedic rep.
Always used humor to disarm tension, build rapport, keep things moving.

COVID brain just made humor functional.

It gave people a script.
It gave me cover.
It made the pause easier to survive.

That helped me.

It probably helped them more.

That was fine.

It kept the room moving.

But humor only works in public.

In private, it was different.

When it happened alone, it was harder to dismiss.

There is no audience to soften it.
No room to redirect.
No joke to bridge the silence.

Just the interruption.

And the private recognition that something in your mind is no longer behaving the way it used to.

That part was harder.

Losing oxygen in public would have been easier to tolerate than losing my train of thought in private.

That was the truth.

The oxygen was visible.
Explainable.
External.

COVID brain was worse because it lived inside the one thing I had always trusted most.

My own mind.

That was harder to absorb than weakness ever was.

And the hand tremors made that harder to dismiss.

The tremors were different.

They were not constant.
Not daily.
Not always visible.

But frequent enough to remind me something in the wiring had changed.

When they showed up, they made simple things harder.

Typing.
Writing.
Holding steady.

Not catastrophic.

Just enough to remind me the deficit was still active.

That mattered.

It made the cognitive part harder to write off as temporary.

The tremors were proof something still lingered.

They gave me Propranolol for it.

It helped.

I hated how it made me feel.

So I stopped.

Wine or alcohol settled the tremors better than anything else ever did.

That is not treatment.

It is just the truth.

Mostly, I learned to live with it.

That became the larger lesson.

Invisible damage does not become less real because no one else can see it.

That was what COVID brain taught me.

The deficit was there whether anyone recognized it or not.

Whether they noticed the pause or not.
Whether they saw the tremor or not.
Whether they understood the apology or not.

It was there.

Active.
Present.
Invisible.

That was the hardest kind of recovery.

Not because it hurt more.

Because it had to be explained.

Weakness was visible.

COVID brain was worse, because I had to explain what no one else could see.

PART IV — WHAT REMAINED

20. What It Cost

COVID took more than my lungs.

That was the first lie recovery tries to tell.

It makes the damage look singular.
Respiratory.
Clinical.
Contained.

It wasn't.

COVID did not just take my breath.

It took endurance.
It took certainty.
It took time.
It took trust in my body.
It took trust in my mind.
It took pieces of the life I had built and forced me to decide which ones were worth carrying back.

That was the real cost.

Physically, the greatest loss was endurance.

More than strength.
More than weight.
More than the mechanics of learning how to walk again.

Strength came back.

Endurance was more expensive.

That was the real physical tax.

Strength can be rebuilt in moments.
Endurance has to be earned back in repetition.

That took longer.

And it cost more.

That was the part I felt everywhere.

Not just in the stairs.
Not just in the shower.
Not just in the first weeks home.

In all of it.

The physical lesson was simple.

It is one thing to survive.

It is another to sustain.

That was the cost.

Mentally, the greatest loss was certainty.

Not competence.

That distinction matters.

I still knew what I knew.
Still knew how to work.
Still knew how to move through conversations, solve problems, navigate complexity, and do the work I had spent years learning to do.

What COVID took was certainty.

The confidence that the thought would arrive when I needed it.
The confidence that the sentence would stay intact long enough to finish it.
The confidence that the sharpest tool I had always relied on—my own mind—would behave on command.

That was the real mental cost.

Not intelligence.

Trust.

That was harder to rebuild.

The hospital bill was over $250,000.

That number should have been terrifying.

It wasn't.

Not really.

By then, the bill was abstract.

The cost was already personal.

I knew it would be high.

That was the point of having health insurance.

The number was surprising only because it gave scale to something I had already lived through.

Luckily, insurance covered most of it.

Friends started a GoFundMe and raised about $5,000 to help cover what remained.

That mattered.

Not just financially.

It mattered because it was one more reminder that while I was unconscious, other people had been carrying parts of my life I couldn't.

That is its own kind of debt.

COVID cost my family the possibility of losing me.

That was the real bill.

Not the hospital.
Not the insurance.
Not the deductible.

The possibility that my wife would have become a widow.
That my kids would have become the people who tell the story of when their father didn't come home.

That was the cost they carried while I was sedated enough not to understand any of it.

That is a debt I did not pay.

They did.

I was lucky.

That is the cleanest version of that truth.

I was lucky.

COVID did not expose weakness in my marriage.

It exposed strength.

That mattered.

Not because Amber became something new.

Because she didn't.

That was the point.

She had always been my rock.
Always been my caregiver.
Always been my companion.

COVID did not reveal something absent.

It put a spotlight on what had been there the whole time.

There is a difference.

She did not become the person who carried me.

She had always been that person.

COVID just stripped enough away to make it impossible to miss.

That mattered.

Confidence was tested.

Not destroyed.

That distinction matters too.

COVID brain did not break confidence as much as it forced adaptation.

I learned to compensate.
Learned to set expectations.
Learned how to work around the lag.
Learned how to keep moving through the deficit without pretending it was not there.

That was not defeat.

That was adjustment.

And adjustment is its own kind of competence.

Most of me came back.

That is true.

Almost all of it.

Everything except full trust that my mind will arrive exactly when I call for it.
Everything except the occasional tremor that still reminds me something in the wiring changed.

That is what never fully returned.

Not function.

Certainty.

That is a different loss.

And a harder one to explain.

Everything important survived.

That matters most.

My marriage survived.
My family survived.
My faith survived.
My perspective survived.
My life survived.

That is not small.

That is everything.

I do not know how to explain that without sounding too simple, but simplicity is probably the cleanest version of the truth.

Everything that actually mattered survived.

That is not the same thing as saying nothing was lost.

A great deal was lost.

But not the things I should have been protecting most.

That was the correction.

The most expensive loss was time.

Time already spent wrong.
Time given too freely to things that were never going to love me back.
Time handed to work.
Time spent away.
Time missed.
Time assumed.

That was the real cost.

And it still is.

That is the only loss still compounding.

COVID took a great deal from me.

But what it exposed cost more than what it took.

It showed me what I had been spending my life on.
What had been worth it.
What had not.
What would still be there if everything stopped.
What wouldn't.

That is not loss.

That is accounting.

And what it left me with was something far more valuable than the life I nearly lost.

It left me with the chance to take it back.

To reprioritize my family.
To move work where it belonged.
Not gone.
Not irrelevant.
Just no longer at the center.

That was the gift inside the cost.

COVID took a great deal from me.

What it left behind mattered more.

21. Who Showed Up

Crisis clarifies people faster than comfort ever will.

That was one of the cleaner lessons.

Illness has a way of stripping relationships down to action.

Not intention.
Not history.
Not what people say they would do.
Not what you assume years of proximity should mean.

Action.

Who called.
Who checked in.
Who showed up.
Who carried weight.
Who disappeared.
Who became louder in absence than they had ever been in presence.

That was the sorting.

And it was cleaner than I expected.

Some people showed up exactly where I thought they would.

Family.
The people closest to me.
The ones whose names were never in question.

That mattered.

Some friends showed up too.

A few old ones.
A few unexpected ones.

A few acquaintances who stepped forward in ways I would not have predicted.

That mattered too.

And then there was the silence.

That was louder than all of it.

Not from strangers.
Not from people I barely knew.
Not from the edges of life where absence is easy to explain.

From people I expected.

That was the part that stayed with me.

Not anger.

Clarity.

That distinction matters.

I was not angry.

I was surprised.
In some cases shocked.
In others, not shocked at all—just finally forced to stop pretending I expected more than they had ever really shown me.

That was the difference.

The silence did not create disappointment.

It removed illusion.

That was more useful.

Some people were not absent because they were cruel.

They were absent because they were occupied by their own lives.

That is not always malicious.

Sometimes it is just reality.

But reality still teaches.

And what it taught me was simple:

Do not confuse familiarity with loyalty.
Do not confuse proximity with presence.
Do not confuse history with investment.

That was the lesson.

Amber never needed a crisis to prove who she was.

That mattered.

COVID did not reveal something new in her.

It just removed any room to miss what had always been true.

Amber is my rock.

That had been true before COVID.
It was just impossible to overlook afterward.

She had the oxygen set up before I ever came home.

Not after.
Not once we figured it out.
Before.

By the time I walked through the door, what I needed was already there.

That mattered more than people realize.

There is love in comfort.
There is love in words.
There is love in concern.

There is another kind in preparation.

That was Amber.

She was already solving problems I had not yet reached.

That is a different kind of care.

Jake became something different in my absence.

That was not subtle.

He thought I was going to die.

That is hard enough.

He was twenty-one.

That part matters.

He dropped out of college and came home.

Not as a gesture.
Not dramatically.
Because in his mind, there was no version of events where being somewhere else made sense.

He came home because he thought his father was dying.

And in my absence, he became the man of the house.

That is too much weight for a twenty-one-year-old.

But he carried it anyway.

That mattered.

Lauren became the bridge between where I was and the world I was still trying to get back to.

That mattered more than I knew at the time.

By the time she came into my room, she was not just my daughter.

She was the first real emotional tether I had to my life outside that room.

That was the difference.

She was not just family.

She was proof my world still existed beyond the walls I had been trapped inside.

And she had to force her way in to do it.

Lauren had just graduated nursing school and was working at UAB.

She went to the head of Nursing and got permission to come see me when no one else could.

That was not small.

That visit grounded me.

More than that, it gave me something none of the machines in that room could.

Connection.

Recognition.
Emotion.
Reality.

If Lauren had not come to see me, I do not know if I would have made it.

That was the turning point.

David V. is the reason I made it to the hospital in time to survive at all.

That matters.

He did not convince me.

He insisted.

There is a difference.

I was not looking for reassurance.
I was looking for permission to minimize what was happening.

He did not give it to me.

He pushed.

That mattered.

Sometimes the people who show up are the ones who refuse to let you make the wrong call.

David was one of them.

Kurtis showed up from a distance in the most practical way possible.

That mattered too.

He was in Huntsville.

He was not physically there.

He was still in the room.

He called daily.
Spoke to my nurses.
Tracked what mattered.

Made sure they were proning me.
Made sure they were protecting my kidneys.
Made sure the right things were being watched by people who did not know me beyond the room number.

That mattered.

Distance does not mean absence when someone chooses otherwise.

Kurtis made sure of that.

Some of the quietest support came from people who never made it about themselves.

That mattered most.

Friends from baseball quietly set up a GoFundMe to help with medical bills.

That mattered.

Not because of the money.

The money helped.

That was not the point.

The point was what it meant.

It was emotional proof.

Proof that someone had seen what was happening and decided to carry part of it without needing attention for doing so.

That mattered more than the amount ever could.

The meal train mattered for the same reason.

It was practical.
It was useful.
It was needed.

But more than that, it was evidence.

Evidence that while my family was carrying the heaviest part, other people had stepped in to make sure they did not carry all of it alone.

That mattered.

One of the biggest surprises came from a business colleague in Mobile.

Not a close friend.
Not someone woven into daily life.
Not someone I would have expected to move beyond professional courtesy.

We knew each other.
Passed in halls.
Knew of one another.
That was about the extent of it.

And still, they showed up.

Quietly.
Without performance.
Without making it bigger than it needed to be.

They sent an Italian meal through the meal train.

A small thing.

A meaningful one.

That was the surprise.

Not because it was large.

Because it was thoughtful.

That stayed.

The people who showed up taught me who mattered.

The people who didn't taught me just as much.

22. What They Carried

While I was unconscious, my family was not.

That was the divide.

It is easy to write about survival from the position of the person who almost died.

It is harder to account for what survival costs the people who had to stay awake through it.

I was sedated.
Intubated.
Removed from the sharpest edges of what was happening.

They were not.

That was the difference.

While I was unconscious enough not to carry it, my family carried all of it for me.

That was the real burden.

Amber carried more than fear.

She carried guilt.

That was heavier.

Fear is immediate.
Fear belongs to uncertainty.
Fear belongs to the moment in front of you.

Guilt lingers.

Guilt rewrites.
Guilt replays.
Guilt asks different questions and offers no relief.

What if we had done more?
What if we had acted sooner?
What if we had pushed harder?
What if the vaccine had changed it?
What if monoclonal antibodies had changed it?
What if ivermectin had changed it?
What if some other decision had altered the outcome before it ever became this?

That was the weight she carried.

Not because she failed.

Because guilt does not require failure to survive.

It only requires love and hindsight.

That burden did not leave when I came home.

Parts of it never fully did.

She still carries some of it now.

That is the cost of surviving something you had no control over and still feeling responsible for how it unfolded.

Amber carried more than my illness.

She carried the infrastructure around it.

Once she recovered enough to function, she became the point of contact for everything.

Updates.
Decisions.
Communication.
Family.
Friends.
Medical information.
The version of events everyone else needed in order to understand what was happening.

She became the central line between the room I was in and the people waiting outside it.

That is its own burden.

She was not just trying to survive what was happening to me.

She was translating it for everyone else.

And she was doing it while trying to survive it herself.

That mattered.

She also had to become everything else at once.

Wife.
Mother.
Caregiver.
Communicator.
Financial operator.
Household anchor.

All at once.

That is too much for one person.

She carried it anyway.

That was the cost.

The kids carried something different.

Not less.

Just different.

They carried fear.
They carried uncertainty.
They carried helplessness.

And unlike me, they had to carry all three while fully conscious.

They were not children.

They were old enough to understand what was happening.

That made it harder.

They were old enough to understand what ventilators meant.
Old enough to understand what COVID was doing.
Old enough to understand what it meant when they could not see me because hospital protocol would not allow it.

That kind of helplessness has weight.

They knew enough to understand the danger.

And not enough to do anything about it.

That was the burden.

They could not fix it.
Could not see me.
Could not intervene.
Could not change what was happening.

All they could do was wait.

That is its own kind of suffering.

The uncertainty was not mine to carry then.

It was theirs.

That is what hindsight makes impossible to miss.

While I was sedated enough not to understand what was happening, they were fully awake inside the possibility that I might not come home.

That was the reality they had to function inside.

Not collapse.
Not pause.
Not step outside of it.

Function.

That is what survival cost them that it did not cost me.

They had to keep moving while waiting to see whether I lived.

That is a different kind of endurance.

They had to keep the house functioning.
Keep bills paid.
Keep the family moving.
Keep communication open.
Keep people informed.
Keep the practical parts of life from collapsing while the emotional center of it was in question.

That was not small.

I handled the bills.

I handled what was on autopay.
What was paid online.
What was due.
What moved where.
What had to be touched and when.

Then I disappeared into a hospital bed.

That burden did not disappear with me.

It transferred.

Amber had to carry the household while learning in real time how much of it had been invisible until it became hers.

That was part of the cost too.

Not just grief.

Infrastructure.

That is the kind of burden people rarely account for because it does not look emotional from the outside.

It is.

It is the emotional cost of practical weight.

And it is heavy.

They also had to protect me from chaos while living inside it.

That part matters.

I was unaware.

That was mercy.

They did not have that luxury.

They had to absorb the uncertainty.
Absorb the fear.
Absorb the logistics.
Absorb the questions.
Absorb the possibility of loss.

And then keep functioning anyway.

That was the work.

That was what they carried.

What I understand now that I could not understand then is simple.

They were surviving my illness too.

Not medically.

But completely.

And in many ways, they had to survive the sharpest parts of it without the mercy sedation gave me.

That is the part hindsight makes unavoidable.

I survived COVID.

My family survived the possibility that I wouldn't.

23. What Stayed

When enough gets stripped away, what remains gets easier to see.

That was the final lesson.

COVID took enough from me to make the math simpler.

It removed noise.
Removed motion.

Removed distraction.
Removed the illusion that everything I had been carrying deserved equal weight.

What stayed was what mattered enough to survive the stripping.

That was the point.

I was still here.

That is where all of it begins.

After the ventilator.
After the Remdesivir.
After the sedation.
After the oxygen.
After the hospitalization.
After the months of recovery.

I was still here.

That mattered more than anything else.

Before anything was rebuilt, before anything was reframed, before priorities were reordered or perspective was corrected, that was the first truth that remained.

I was still here.

That was not small.

That was everything.

Some parts of me made it through untouched.

That surprised me.

Humor stayed.

That mattered.

It carried me through conversations when precision failed.
It gave me cover when COVID brain made pauses visible.
It gave other people a way to stay comfortable while I adjusted to a version of myself I was still learning to work around.

Humor survived intact.

So did faith.

Not in the performative sense.
Not in the polished language people use when they want suffering to sound cleaner than it was.

Faith stayed because there were too many moments it had to.

Too many nights where certainty was gone.
Too many moments where control was gone.
Too many outcomes I did not own.

Faith remained because some part of me needed something larger than prognosis to stand on.

That stayed.

Drive stayed too.

Just not in the same direction.

That was the difference.

The drive to build.
The drive to move.
The drive to create.
The drive to matter.

That survived.

What changed was where it pointed.

Before COVID, I was a workaholic.

That is the cleanest version of it.

Work was not just what I did.

It was what I measured myself against.

Output.
Productivity.
Income.
Movement.
Being needed.
Being useful.
Being busy enough to justify absence.

That was the old math.

After COVID, that version lost rank.

Not because work stopped mattering.

Because it stopped outranking everything else.

That was the permanent change.

Work did not lose meaning.

It lost priority.

That is different.

And permanent.

Family did not become more important.

COVID just forced everything else to finally fall beneath it.

That was the correction.

Family had always mattered most.

COVID just removed enough illusion to make pretending otherwise impossible.

That was the shift.

That was what stayed.

Not just my family.

My understanding of what they were worth.

That changed permanently.

Time changed too.

Or maybe more accurately, my relationship to it did.

Time became harder to waste.

Not impossible.

But harder.

I protect it differently now.

I try to protect it better.

Not perfectly.

But intentionally.

Time without purpose costs more now than it used to.

Time spent wrong is easier to feel.
Time spent well is easier to defend.
Time spent with my family is no longer negotiable.

That became fixed.

That stayed.

So did perspective.

Survival did not make me softer.

It made me calmer.

That is different.

I have less appetite for noise now.
Less tolerance for people who waste time, energy, attention, or peace.
Less interest in performance.
Less interest in proving.
Less interest in carrying things that do not deserve the weight.

That is not bitterness.

It is filtration.

That stayed.

What other people think matters less now than it ever has.

That changed permanently too.

Other people's opinions used to carry more weight than they deserved.

They do not now.

That is one of the cleaner gifts suffering leaves behind.

Perspective makes most outside opinions too small to carry.

That stayed.

So did love.

More of it.

Not broader.

Clearer.

I love my family with less distraction now.
With less competition.
With less of myself handed out to things that were never going to love me back.

That changed too.

Not the love.

Its access.

That stayed.

And legacy changed.

Before COVID, success looked like output.
Like growth.
Like movement.
Like accumulation.
Like proving.

After COVID, legacy looked different.

Less about what I built.
More about what remains after me.

That changed everything.

I think more now about what survives me than what impresses people while I am here.

That is a better metric.

That stayed.

Who I was after all of it was not the man I was before it.

That version did not die.

It just lost rank.

What remained was clearer.

I was a survivor.
A husband.
A father.
A mentor.
A philanthropist.

In that order.

That was the reordering.

That was what stayed.

Not the old version of me.

What stayed was what mattered enough to survive being stripped down.

COVID did not leave me unchanged.

It left me clarified.

24. What Comes After

Survival is not the end of the story.

It is the handoff.

That was the final shift.

For a while, surviving is enough.
Breathing is enough.
Getting home is enough.
Walking is enough.

Working is enough.
Getting your life back in working order is enough.

For a while, survival is the whole story.

Then eventually it isn't.

Eventually survival stops being the headline and becomes the responsibility.

That is what comes after.

The question changes.

Not how do I survive this.

What do I do with what survived?

That is a different question.

And it is the more important one.

Surviving gave me something I did not have before.

Not more time.

Clarity.

That mattered more.

It made some things smaller.
It made some things disappear.
It made some things impossible to pretend were still worth the weight I had been giving them.

That was the first correction.

Work got smaller.

Not irrelevant.
Not unimportant.
Not unnecessary.

Smaller.

It stopped being identity.
Stopped being purpose.
Stopped being the thing everything else bent around.

That changed.

And what took its place was not comfort.

It was responsibility.

That is what comes after survival.

Responsibility.

Not just to be grateful.
Not just to appreciate what almost disappeared.
Not just to say it changed me and leave it there.

Responsibility to do something useful with what came back.

That is the real obligation.

A second chance is not just relief.

It is stewardship.

That was the deeper meaning.

I do not believe surviving something like this is meant to end in comfort.

I think it demands usefulness.

That is what changed most.

Before COVID, success had a different shape.

It looked like work.
Income.
Production.
Growth.
Motion.
Building something because building it proved something.

That is not what it looks like now.

Now it looks like service.

That is the shift.

Not away from ambition.

Toward usefulness.

That is different.

What comes after survival is not smaller ambition.

It is better aim.

That is where the work changed.

Not into one thing.

Into purpose.

What I build now is no longer built only to produce.

It is built to serve.

That is the difference.

That is what changed.

The work ahead is no longer just about income.

It is about impact.

It is about building things that outlive me.
Building things that serve people who need more than another transaction.
Building things that lighten burdens instead of adding to them.
Building things with enough permanence to matter after I am gone.

That is the point.

That is what comes after.

Not one project.

A reordering of purpose.

That was the real shift.

Survival did not make me less ambitious.

It made me less interested in ambition that ends with me.

That is different.

I still want to build.

I just no longer care to build things that terminate in income and die there.

That is too small now.

What matters is whether what I build outlives me.
Whether it serves someone beyond me.
Whether it leaves something behind worth having.

That is legacy.

And survival put that in clearer focus than success ever did.

That is what changed.

Financial stewardship matters more now too.

Not because money matters more.

Because burden does.

I do not want my children carrying me one day because I failed to plan while I had time.

That matters.

Being financially stable now is not about accumulation for its own sake.

It is about protection.
It is about stewardship.
It is about making sure the people I love inherit stability, not avoidable weight.

That is different.

That is what responsibility looks like in practice.

Wasting this second chance would be simple.

Go back.
Chase money.
Build nothing larger than comfort.
Spend what is left proving things that no longer matter.
Make work the center again.
Learn nothing.
Offer nothing.
Leave nothing.

That would be waste.

That is no longer acceptable to me.

What deserves the life I got back is simple.

My family.
My work, in its proper place.
The people I can help.
The things I can build that still matter when I am gone.

That is what deserves what came back.

And part of that responsibility is telling the story.

That matters too.

Not because the story is mine.

Because survival is not rare.
Isolation is not rare.
Fear is not rare.
And neither is the lie people tell themselves that if they survive something hard, survival itself is the finish line.

It isn't.

The story matters because what comes after matters.

If survival gives you your life back, the next question is what your life is for.

That is the part worth saying out loud.

What comes after survival is service.

What comes after survival is stewardship.

What comes after survival is deciding that what came back was not just returned.

It was entrusted.

Surviving gave me my life back.

What comes after is proving it was worth being given back at all.

25. Why Tell It

This book is not written to relive what happened.

It is written because too much of what happened disappears the moment people survive it.

That is part of the problem.

The public sees outcomes.
Families see updates.
Charts record numbers.
Hospitals document interventions.

Very little records what it felt like to live through any of it.

Less still records what it cost the people standing outside the room.

That is why this needs to be told.

Not because my story is unique.

Because too much of it isn't.

Too many families have stood outside ICU rooms waiting for updates instead of answers.
Too many people have been reduced to protocols before they were treated like people.
Too many survivors came home alive and were expected to call that the whole story.

It wasn't.

That is why this exists.

This is not just a survival story.

It is a witness statement.

That matters.

I am telling this publicly for a few reasons.

First, because families deserve context for what they lived through.

Not just the patient.

The family.

The people waiting outside.
The people taking calls.
The people carrying uncertainty.
The people living in updates and silence and hospital policy and helplessness.

Families deserve language for what happened to them too.

This gives some of that back.

Second, this is the only way to put the memory somewhere other than my own head.

That matters too.

Some stories stay heavy until they are given somewhere to go.

This is that place.

Part of writing this is for the public.

Part of it is for my family.

And part of it is for me.

My wife.
My children.
The people who carried me.
The people who lived their own version of this while I was sedated enough not to remember it in real time.

They deserve to know what they meant to me from the inside of it.

This gives them that too.

And beyond that, this is the only honest way to tell what survival actually cost.

Not just medically.

Humanly.

That is what I hope someone takes from this.

Comfort.
Context.
Understanding.

Not comfort in the easy sense.

Not reassurance.

Recognition.

The kind that comes from finally having language for something you lived through and never had a clean way to name.

That would make telling this worth it.

If someone reads this and feels less alone in what they carried, it was worth writing.

If a family reads this and better understands what their loved one may have experienced behind sedation, it was worth writing.

If a survivor reads this and sees their own silence reflected back clearly enough to finally name it, it was worth writing.

That is enough.

What I want this story to do is interrupt assumption.

That is the real goal.

Most people think survival ends at discharge.

It doesn't.

Most people think hospital care happens only to the patient.

It doesn't.

Most people think if someone survives, the story resolves.

It doesn't.

That is what this book is meant to interrupt.

Not medicine.

Not care.

Distance.

Protocol without personhood.
Systems without nuance.
Treatment without dignity.
Policy without humanity.

That is the fracture.

And too many people know it only after they have already lived through it.

That is the lie I want dismantled.

Not that medicine fails.

That medicine becomes dangerous the moment the person disappears and only the protocol remains.

People are not interchangeable.
People are not identical.

People are not best served by being reduced to a standard response and managed like a category.

That is not care.

That is administration.

And there is a difference.

People deserve facts.
People deserve context.
People deserve informed decisions.
People deserve to understand what is happening to them and why.
People deserve treatment that sees the person, not just the process.

Blind trust is not informed care.

And too many people were taught to mistake one for the other.

That needs to be said.

Not because medicine is useless.

Because medicine without humanity becomes something else.

This story is not written to assign blame.

It is written to bear witness.

To what survival felt like.
To what families carried.
To what was lost in the distance between treatment and personhood.
To what happens when protocols become louder than people.

That is why this story belongs in print.

And that is why now matters.

Not because the timing is dramatic.

Because people are tired.
Tired of systems that ask for trust and offer distance.
Tired of institutions that ask for compliance and offer abstraction.
Tired of being managed and not seen.

People are looking for something honest.

This is honest.

Not polished.
Not ideological.
Not interested in winning an argument.

Just honest.

And sometimes witness is more useful than certainty.

That is why this story needs to be told now.

Not to prove what happened.

To make sure what happened is no longer easy to ignore.

Photo Insert — What Survival Looked Like

The photographs included in this book are personal images from my hospitalization and recovery. Some are difficult to look at. They are included not for shock value, but because survival has a visible cost, and the camera often told the truth before I fully understood it myself.

They are part of the record.

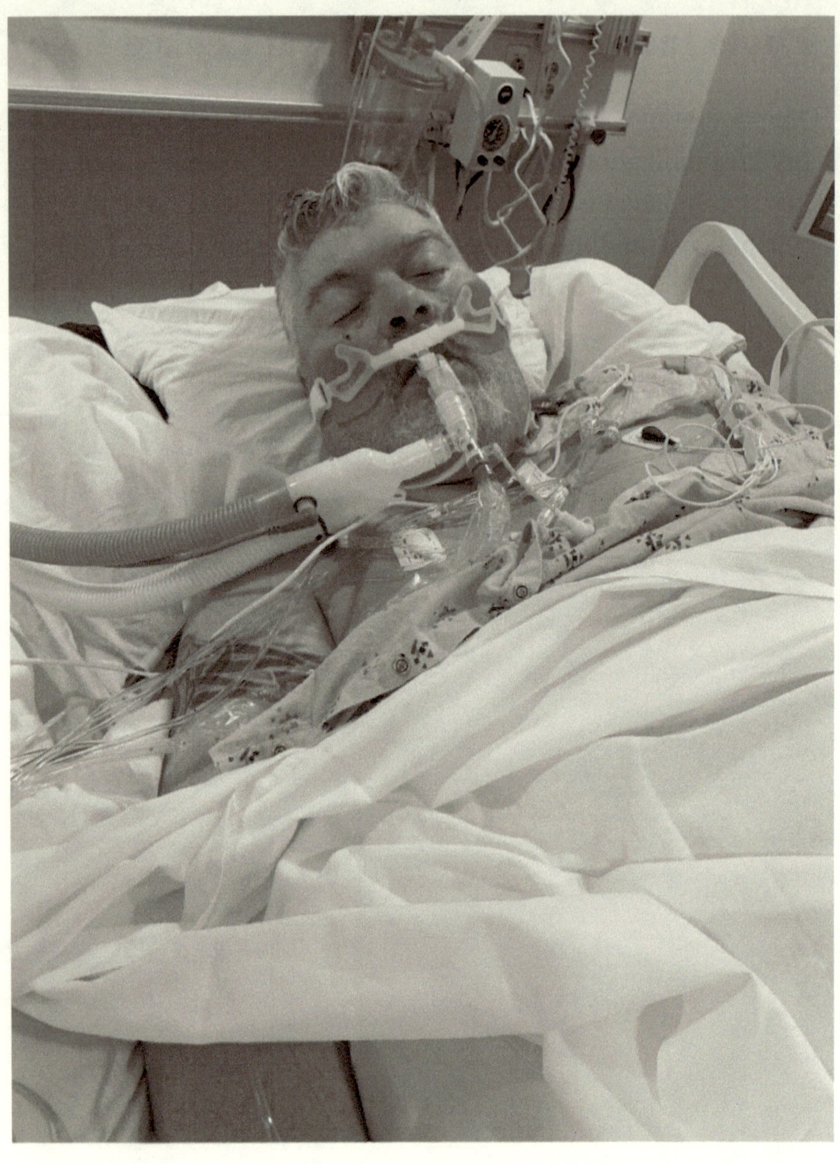

1. Seven days gone. This is the version of me my family had to imagine from outside the room. I do not remember this moment. They do.

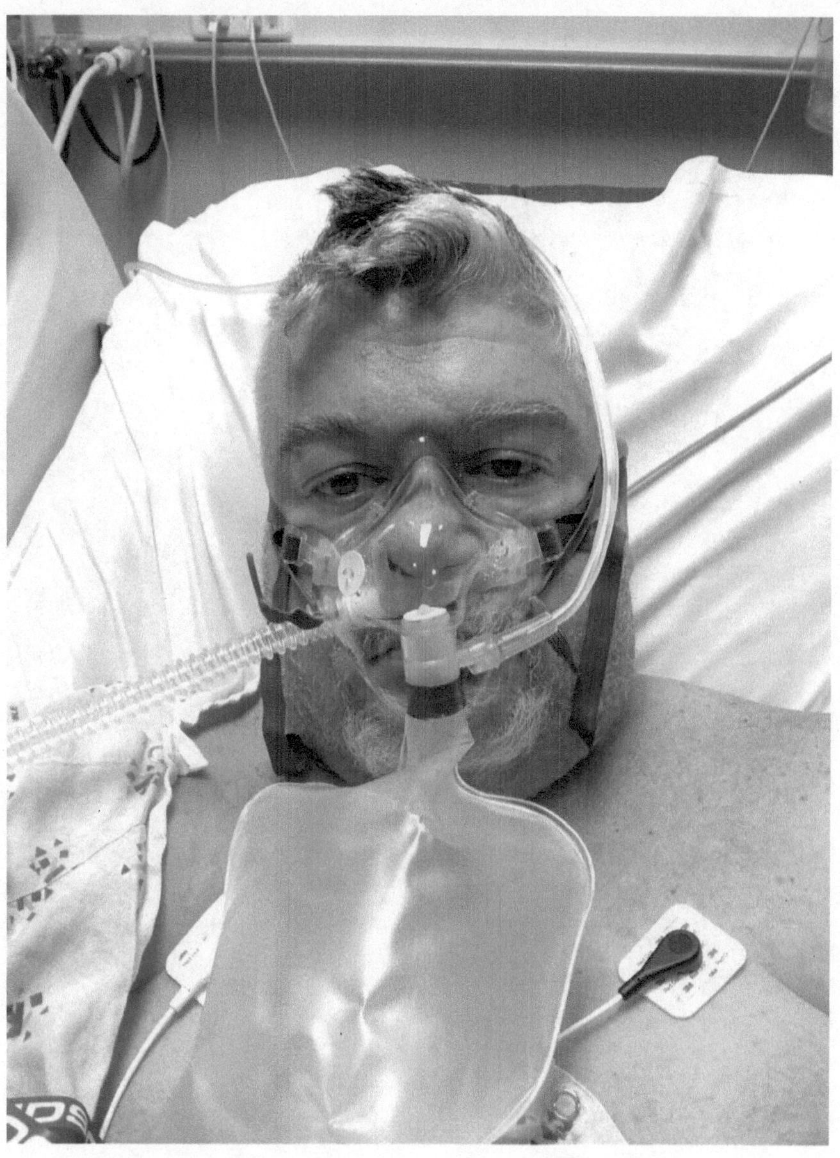

2. Still breathing, but barely. At the time, I thought I was documenting progress. Looking back, the camera was more honest than I was.

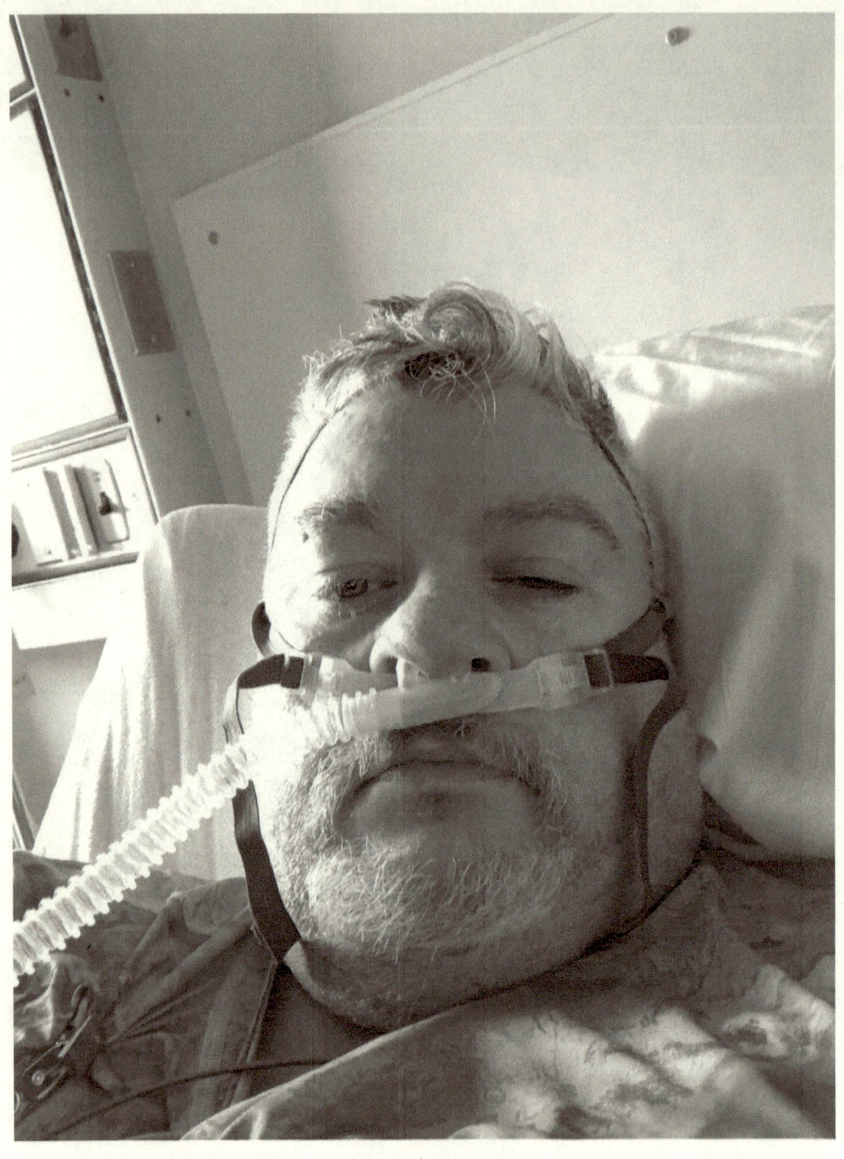

3. The first look back. I recognized my face, but not everything behind my eyes had returned yet.

4. Discharge day. I remember thinking I smiled for this picture. Later, when I saw it, I realized my face had not caught up with what my heart was trying to say. I was alive. I was coming home. But I was not back.

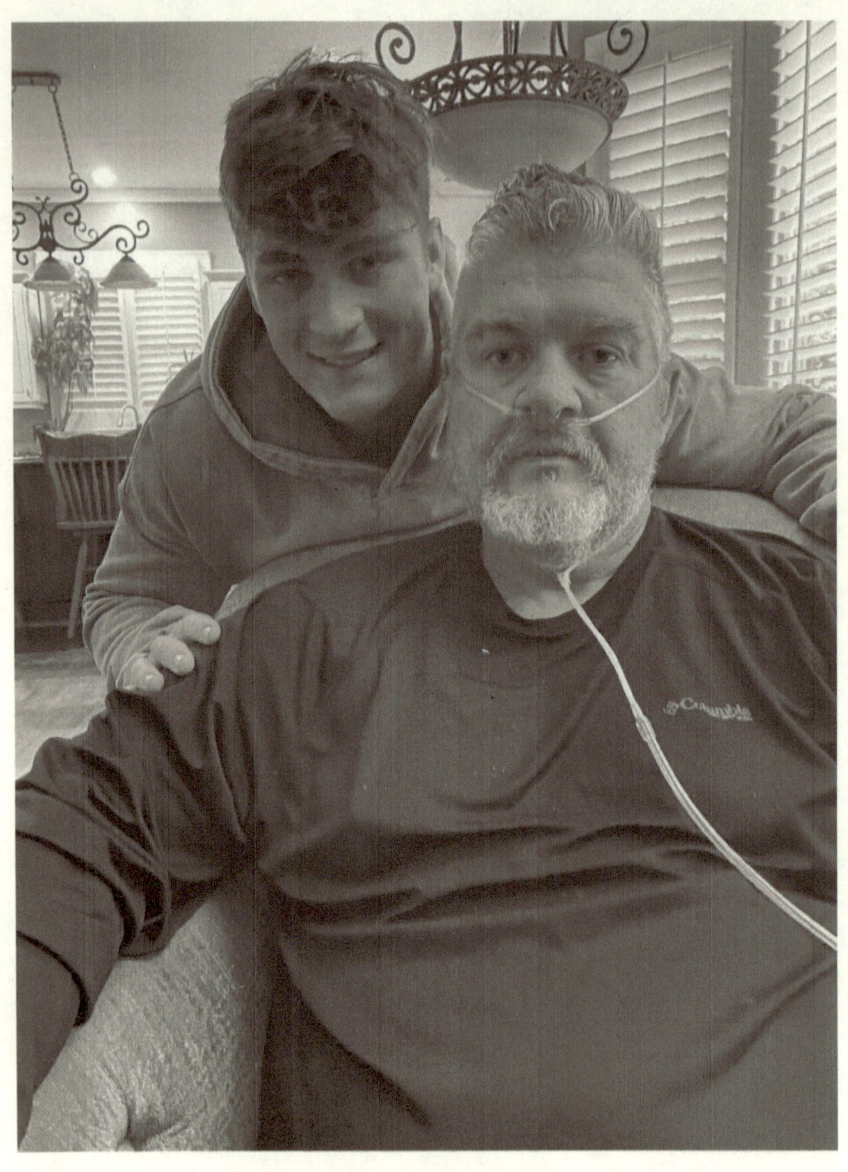

5. Home, but not back. The hospital was behind me, but oxygen still followed me from room to room.

6. Coming back took longer than coming home. Recovery did not happen all at once. It returned in pieces.

7. Freedom Isn't Free. Amber believes this tattoo may have mattered when the last COVID-unit bed became part of our story. I cannot prove that. But I understand why she believes it.

Epilogue — Closing Reflection

Survival is not the clean ending people want it to be.

People like endings that resolve neatly. Illness. Treatment. Recovery. Return. A straight line from suffering back to normal, as if surviving something difficult means life simply resumes where it left off.

It does not.

Survival is not reversal.

You do not come home the way you left.

That is the part people misunderstand most.

The body heals in pieces. Some of it comes back. Some of it does not. Strength returns slowly. Breath returns unevenly. Routine rebuilds itself one small act at a time. Enough of life begins to resemble what it was that, from the outside, people start calling it recovery.

But survival does not return the same person to the same life.

It returns someone altered.

That is not tragedy.
It is consequence.

There are parts of me that never came back.

The part that believed work mattered more than presence.
The part that thought provision and attention were the same thing.
The part that spent too much time focused on what other people thought, on what needed proving, on what looked important from the outside and meant very little in the quiet places where life is actually lived.

That version of me did not survive.

And that is not the loss I mourn.

My family became the clearest truth left standing after everything else was stripped away.

Not abstractly.
Not sentimentally.

Clearly.

Time with them is no longer something I fit around the rest of life.

It is the point of it.

That is what became sacred.

Not achievement.
Not appearances.
Not the endless chase for things that feel urgent until life reminds you they are not.

Work still matters.
Responsibility still matters.
Providing still matters.

But they no longer sit at the center.

They are part of life.

They are not the reason for it.

That distinction cost me enough to learn.

Life does not always break where you expect it to.
And it does not rebuild according to your plan.

It bends.
It interrupts.

It takes shape around loss, around fear, around the things you never asked to carry.

And then, whether you are ready or not, it asks you to keep going.

That is the work.

Not pretending it did not happen.
Not spending the rest of your life trying to become the person you were before it.

The work is learning how to build honestly with what remains.

That is what survival asks of you.

Not perfection.

Not certainty.

Only honesty.
Only perspective.
Only the willingness to stop worshipping what nearly made you miss your life while you were busy building it.

If there is anything worth carrying from this, it is simple:

Life will shape you whether you consent to it or not.

Your task is to decide what that shaping becomes.

No matter how hard life gets, God may have a different path for you.

Acknowledgments

There are people woven into this story so deeply that it would not exist without them.

First, Amber.

You carried more than anyone will ever fully understand. While I was unconscious, you were the one holding everything together—our home, our family, the fear, the uncertainty, and the very real possibility that I might not come home. Then when I did, you carried me through recovery too. You helped me stand. You helped me breathe. You helped me come back. There is no version of this story where I make it through without you. I came home because you never stopped holding the line.

Jake,

You drove me to the hospital. You drove your mother the next day. You had to leave both of us at those doors and walk away not knowing what came next. No son should have to carry that. But you did. And you carried it with strength, with steadiness, and with more grace than I understood at the time. I know what that cost you now. I will never forget it.

Lauren,

You found your way to me when no one else could. You pushed through protocol, through fear, through every barrier between us, and you put your hand in mine when I needed something real to hold onto. You were the first thing that made me believe I was still connected to the world outside that room. You gave me something to fight back toward. I will never be able to fully explain what that meant to me, only that it meant everything.

To my brother Kurtis,

You watched what I could not. You saw what I could not ask about. You paid attention when I had no voice left to use. From a distance, you helped guide my care, asked the harder questions, and made sure someone who understood exactly what was happening was always watching. You helped save my life, and I know that.

David V.,

You were the first person who said what needed to be said. When I still thought I could wait it out, you didn't let me. You told me if I didn't get my ass to the hospital, you'd come drag me there yourself. It was blunt. It was exactly what I needed to hear. That moment changed everything. You were right, and it may very well be one of the reasons I am still here to write this.

To the nurses, doctors, respiratory therapists, and staff who cared for me,

Thank you for the work you do in rooms most people never see and under pressure most people will never understand. You stood in the space between life and death and did the work anyway. Whatever disagreements I may have with parts of the system, I will never fail to respect the people who kept showing up inside it.

To the friends who showed up,

Thank you for the calls, the meals, the prayers, the help, and the quiet ways you made life easier when it mattered most. The people who acted revealed themselves clearly. I have not forgotten what you did.

And finally, to God,

You gave me another chance. Everything after that is gratitude.

Medical Note / Disclaimer

This book is a personal memoir and reflects the author's individual experience with illness, hospitalization, survival, and recovery. It is not intended to provide medical advice, diagnosis, treatment recommendations, or guidance regarding vaccines, medications, hospitalization, oxygen therapy, respiratory care, or any other medical decision.

Every medical situation is different. Readers should consult qualified healthcare professionals regarding their own health, treatment options, and medical decisions.

The events described are remembered and presented from the author's perspective. Some names, identifying details, and timelines may have been condensed or adjusted for privacy and narrative clarity while preserving the truth of the experience.

Photo Credits / Permissions Note

All photographs are from the author's personal collection and are used with permission where applicable. Images are included to document the author's hospitalization, recovery, and return home.

Any medical staff shown or identifiable in photographs should be included only with written permission, or the photograph should be omitted or cropped before publication.

www.ingramcontent.com/pod-product-compliance
Lightning Source LLC
LaVergne TN
LVHW090512110826
845146LV00003B/823

* 9 7 9 8 9 9 6 1 2 5 2 0 3 *